Crime and Punishment in Upper Canada

GENEALOGIST'S REFERENCE SHELF

Crime and Punishment in Upper Canada

JANICE NICKERSON

A Researcher's Guide

DUNDURN PRESS
TORONTO

Editor: Ruth Chernia
Copy editor: Cheryl Hawley
Design: Courtney Horner
Printer: Transcontinental

Library and Archives Canada Cataloguing in Publication

Nickerson, Janice C., 1969-
    Crime and punishment in Upper Canada : a researcher's guide / by Janice Nickerson.

(Genealogist's reference shelf)
Co-published by: Ontario Genealogical Society.
Issued also in electronic format.
ISBN 978-1-55488-770-5

    1. Crime--Ontario--History--Sources. 2. Criminal justice, Administration of--Ontario--History--Sources. 3. Court records--Ontario--Archival resources. 4. Criminal records--Ontario--Archival resources. 5. Crime--Ontario--Archival resources. 6. Criminal justice, Administration of--Ontario--Archival resources. 7. Upper Canada--Archival resources. 8. Ontario--Archival resources. 9. Ontario--Genealogy--Handbooks, manuals, etc. I. Ontario Genealogical Society II. Title. III. Series: Genealogist's reference shelf

HV6809.O6N53 2010   364.971309'034   C2010-902406-0

1   2   3   4   5   14   13   12   11   10

 Conseil des Arts du Canada   Canada Council for the Arts   Canada   ONTARIO ARTS COUNCIL CONSEIL DES ARTS DE L'ONTARIO

We acknowledge the support of the **Canada Council for the Arts** and the **Ontario Arts Council** for our publishing program. We also acknowledge the financial support of the **Government of Canada** through the **Canada Book Fund** and **The Association for the Export of Canadian Books**, and the **Government of Ontario** through the **Ontario Book Publishers Tax Credit program**, and the **Ontario Media Development Corporation**.

Care has been taken to trace the ownership of copyright material used in this book. The author and the publisher welcome any information enabling them to rectify any references or credits in subsequent editions.

J. Kirk Howard, President

Printed and bound in Canada.
www.dundurn.com

Ontario Genealogical Society
Suite 102, 40 Orchard View Boulevard
Toronto, Ontario, Canada M4R 1B9
tel. (416) 489-0734   fax. (416) 489-9803
provoffice@ogs.on.ca   www.ogs.on.ca

Dundurn Press	Gazelle Book Services Limited	Dundurn Press
3 Church Street, Suite 500	White Cross Mills	2250 Military Road
Toronto, Ontario, Canada	High Town, Lancaster, England	Tonawanda, NY
M5E 1M2	LA1 4XS	U.S.A. 14150

CONTENTS

PREFACE

The idea for this book was conceived as I struggled to understand the morass of records created by the Upper Canadian justice system in my work as a professional genealogist.

I was faced with a project in which a client's ancestor had been accused of criminal activity. How could I find out more? Where should I look? The answers were not easy to find. And as I began examining the original records, I found them difficult to understand because I didn't know enough about the way the justice system worked. I didn't know who the personnel were, why they created the records they did, and how to locate those records that survived. I gradually came to believe that a guide for other researchers was needed.

Foremost in my mind were genealogists seeking to learn about their own ancestors' brushes with the law. However, researchers in other historical fields may also find it useful to have information about the entire system of justice in Upper Canada and its records gathered in one place.

This is not a typical genealogist's guide, in that it is only partly about the records. I have found that in order to locate and understand the records it is necessary to understand their context. So, the large part of this book is about the history of the criminal justice system in Upper Canada. I walk the reader through the criminal justice process, step-by-step, explaining who did what, and what records were created in the process. As I discuss the process I illustrate it with examples of original records. I've also provided an inventory of available records to assist the reader in determining which records are available for which location and time period. Each section also contains mini-case studies featuring the stories of real people whose lives were somehow touched by the justice system — as victims, criminals, witnesses, investigators, adjudicators, and administrators.

I have chosen to restrict my focus to the Upper Canada period, that is the years from 1791 to 1841. There are several reasons for this: First, this period is the formative one for the region that eventually became the province of Ontario. Understanding how the system began is critical to understanding later developments. While I considered expanding the period to cover the entire nineteenth century, I found that there were so many changes during the post-1841 period that it would be difficult to explain them all without confusing the reader. Second, with the growth in population came necessary expansions in the justice system, along with an exponential increase in the number and kinds of available records. It would be difficult to describe them all within the confines of a handy guide.

I have also limited myself to the criminal justice system. I have not included information about civil, probate, and equity courts, nor have I gone into any detail about the administrative functions of the courts that also handled criminal justice. However, I have defined criminal loosely. That is, I have included the treatment of misdemeanors and by-law infractions. Also, in my discussion of imprisonment, I have included information about other uses of the gaols (jails), such as the incarceration of debtors and the mentally ill.

ABBREVIATIONS USED

The acronyms at the beginning of each item in the records inventories refer to the following repositories:

AO: Archives of Ontario
BULA: Brock University Library Archives
HCM: Huron County Museum and Historic Gaol
LSUC: Law Society of Upper Canada
LAC: Library and Archives Canada
MUML: McMaster University, Mills Memorial Library, William Ready Division of Archives Research Collection
NHS: Norfolk Historical Society
PCMA: Peterborough Centennial Museum and Archives
QUA: Queen's University Archives
TCA: Toronto City Archives
TPL: Toronto Public Library, Baldwin Room
TUA: Trent University Archives
UWO: University of Western Ontario Library, Archives and Research Collections Centre

CHAPTER ONE

The Context

Upper Canada was a sparsely populated British colony with an extremely low crime rate.[1] Public institutions were primitive and most people had their hands full clearing and cultivating their newly acquired land, and trying to keep their pigs from wandering off. It wasn't a coincidence that the first recorded topic discussed at a meeting of the inhabitants of York concerned fences to corral pigs.[2]

Nonetheless, even an infant colony needed a justice system. Upper Canada's system was intended to be an exact duplicate of Britain's. But, of course, local conditions required some modifications. The important thing was to avoid making the perceived mistakes that had lead to the American Revolution.

Thus, from the very beginning, Upper Canadians defined themselves explicitly as "not American." What made them different was loyalty.[3] Virtually every political issue ended up being about who was loyal and who wasn't.

In 1791 the majority of the European inhabitants were United Empire Loyalists — refugees from the American Revolution who had stayed loyal to the King and the British Empire. They believed

Log Cabin, T. H. Ware, 1844. The original image is part of the Orilliana historical collection at the Orillia Public Library.

that the British constitution provided the most freedom and happiness possible in a peaceful and moral society.[4] They feared unchecked democracy and the separation of church and state because they believed that democracy tempted politicians to play upon the worst appetites of man, and without official sanction the church would lose the moral authority to keep public order. They were convinced this would encourage greed, crime, and violence.[5]

Their political masters were colonial officials whose own ideas of loyalty included fierce adherence to the "beliefs and institutions they considered essential to the preservation of a form of life superior to the manners, politics and social arrangements of the United States." These included the supremacy of the Anglican Church, a hereditary aristocracy, and a balanced constitution. With those elements in place they believed that the Upper Canadian government would ensure that society was stable, orderly, peaceful, and respectable.[6] To put it mildly, Upper Canada was an extremely conservative society.

It was also politically repressive.[7] Criticism of the government or its officers was not permitted.[8] Political offices were filled through a system of patronage that took almost no account of experience or knowledge. The key requirement for any office was loyalty.[9]

However, one of the principles that the British were so proud of was the centrality of the rule of law in the constitution. This meant that the law was above everyone and applied to everyone equally.[10]

Tension between these two values — the importance of loyalty and the rule of law — would lead to many legal battles over the course of the fifty years of Upper Canadian history. For example, because the Attorney General and the Solicitor General claimed the monopoly on prosecutions at the Assizes rather than allowing the victim to hire counsel to conduct the prosecution, as in Britain, but still retained the right to private practice, sometimes they ended up prosecuting a man in the criminal court and defending him in the civil court.

New political ideas and social struggles were introduced by successive waves of immigrants to the colony. Between 1791 and 1812, the majority of the new arrivals were from the United States. Thus, of approximately 80,000 people in Upper Canada in 1812, about 60 percent were born in the United States.[11] This inevitably led to worries about the loyalty of the population, and restrictions on immigration from the United States following the War of 1812, which had nearly resulted in Upper Canada becoming an American state.

Between 1812 and 1841, the majority of the immigrants to Upper Canada were from the British Isles: England, Scotland, and Ireland. By 1842, Upper Canada's population had increased to 487,053. Of those, 54 percent were Canadian born, 7 percent were born in the United States, 33 percent were born in the

British Isles, 1 percent were born in Europe. The remaining 5 percent did not have a place of birth specified in the census.[12]

One of the important effects of huge increase in population was to dilute the proportion of the population that adhered to the Anglican Church. By 1842, only 22 percent of Upper Canadian residents were Anglican. Seventeen percent belonged to one of the many Methodist denominations; 16 percent belonged to the Church of Scotland; 13 percent belonged to the Roman Catholic Church; 4 percent belonged to other Presbyterian denominations; 3 percent belonged to the Baptist Church; 1 percent belonged to each of the Congregational Church, Lutheran Church, and Society of Friends (Quaker); 5 percent belonged to other denominations; and 17 percent did not state a religion in the census.[13] Naturally, special privileges for the Anglican Church became a major bone of contention. Members of other religious denominations resented the fact that their taxes went to support the salaries of Anglican ministers (and not those of other denominations) and Anglican churches were built on land specially reserved for them by the government. This was only one of the issues that led up to the Rebellion of 1837, but it was a key one.

Morality, Criminality, and Justice

In a deeply conservative society such as Upper Canada, crime was considered a natural extension of immorality. If the community was made up of morally upstanding citizens there would be no crime. But if immorality were to gain a foothold, crime would surely follow. So it was important to enforce moral behaviour. Hence, breaking the Sabbath and blasphemy were indictable offences.[14] And other kinds of moral order offences, such as drunk and disorderly, vagrancy, public nuisance, and prostitution landed people in gaol (jail) nearly as often as offences we might today consider criminal.

Newspaper editors often discussed the "problem" of crime and its causes and solutions. It was generally believed that a small minority of people were innately "depraved."[15] But the main causes of crime boiled down to idleness (laziness, not working hard), drunkenness (which was both caused by and led to idleness), and lack of moral education (which led to both idleness and drunkenness).[16] Thus, one of the more frequent suggestions for curbing crime was to encourage religious instruction to help people learn how to curb their baser instincts.[17] Another was to limit the number of tavern licences and to appoint innkeepers as constables — with responsibility of keeping their patrons from becoming drunk and disorderly.[18] Finally, there were attempts to find work for people while in gaol or prison — to help them learn industrious habits (and help pay for their keep, of course).[19]

Inequality Before the Law

Other factors were also at play when Upper Canadians thought about crime. Then, just as now, there were ethnic and racial tensions. The black population was extremely small, perhaps 3 percent, but young black males were often targeted as suspects in theft cases, and when victims were black, fines and other punishments were very low compared to when victims were white.[20]

Then, as now, some people thought minorities were treated too leniently. In 1842 a letter to the editor published in the *Brantford Courier* opined,

> It is high time that the majesty of the law should be vindicated as regards Indians and negroes. Really the government has been too lenient to

both these classes of men in Canada; for of late years it was found to be sufficient reason to be an Indian or Negro to escape the gallows, no matter what crime they may have committed; whilst in too many instances white men were punished with all the rigours of the law.[21]

A much larger "racial" problem was presented by the Irish, especially in urban areas in the 1830s, when immigration from Ireland (especially Roman Catholics) was at its peak.[22] Judging by newspaper editorials, the Irish were believed to be ruled by "untamed animal instincts" (thus accounting for the frequency with which they got into fights). The rhetoric of the period wasn't so different from today's; only the target has changed. Some of the complaints about the Irish included:

- They clustered in poor neighbourhoods;
- They had low morals;
- They had high rates of single parent families; and
- they got involved in gangs.

The Irish were disproportionately represented in justice records, especially for "moral order" offences such as being drunk and disorderly, vagrancy, public nuisance, and prostitution.[23] The number of Irish who spent time in the Hamilton gaol between 1832 and 1843 was significantly out of proportion to the population (the Irish-born represented 35 percent of gaol population when only 12 percent of the population was Irish-born) — especially young Irish Roman Catholic women (60 percent of all women in gaol between 1831 and 1851 were Irish). Irish women stood out even more among those gaoled for public order offences. Of the women taken in for drunk and disorderly conduct, three quarters were Irish; of those taken in for vagrancy, four-fifths were Irish.[24]

Comparison of Country of Origin of Jail Population with That of Gore District Population[25]

Country of Origin	Distribution of Jail Population, 1832–1843	Distribution of District Population, 1842
England and Wales	14 %	13 %
Ireland	35 %	12 %
Scotland	6 %	12 %
Upper Canada	26 %	56 %
United States	17 %	7 %

Sexism was also a pervasive factor in everyday life as well as in the justice system. Women could not vote or hold any office. Married women could not own property. Wife beating was almost never reported, unless the wife feared for her life. Even then, there were very few convictions. Rape was treated more like property damage (the true victim being the woman's father or husband) than violent assault. A husband could not rape his wife, partly because marriage created one legal person and partly because marriage implied permanent consent.[26]

A newspaper article printed in 1834 summarized the rights of wives thus:

> The effects produced by marriage, on the legal rights of the parties are important to be known in every family.
>
> In law husband and wife are considered as one person; and on this principle all civil duties, and disabilities rest.
>
> The wife cannot sue in her own name.
>
> If she suffers injury or wrong in her person

or property, she can with her husband's aid and concurrence prosecute for redress; but the husband must always be the plaintiff. In criminal cases, however, the relation assumes a new form. The wife may, in criminal cases be prosecuted and punished.[27]

Crime and Criminal Law

The laws of Upper Canada were very harsh. When Upper Canada was founded as a colony, its first legislative action was to adopt all the laws of England for the colony. Some laws were later modified, but only very gradually. Even after a new statute was passed in 1833 to reduce the number of capital crimes, there were still many crimes punishable by death: treason (three types), murder, rescuing persons convicted of murder or committed for murder, rape, carnal knowledge of a girl under the age of ten, sodomy, robbery, burglary, arson, rioting, burning or destroying his majesty's ships, arsenals, magazines of naval or military stores, accessory before the fact to any capital offence. [28]

Crimes Against Persons

This category includes abduction, assault, beating, cutting, kidnapping, murder, shooting, and stabbing. In his study of the Gore District gaol records, John Weaver calculated the average rate of crimes against persons between 1832 and 1840 as 75 per 100,000.[30] By comparison, the 2006 rate for violent crime in Ontario was 756.

Crimes Against Persons Prosecuted
in the Niagara District[29]

	Assault at Quarter Sessions	Assault at Assizes	Murder at Assizes
1828	35	0	0
1829	30	1	0
1830	52	0	1
1831	43	0	0
1832	39	0	1
1833	62	0	1
1834	17	1	0
1835	12	0	1
1836	5	0	6
1837	8	0	0
1838	8	1	0
1839	4	6	1
1840	6	3	1
1841	7	1	1

Assault was the most common offence by far in the Upper Canada period. In the Niagara District there were 261 cases of assault at the Quarter Sessions (the lower court) from 1828 to 1833. However, only one was severe enough to be prosecuted at the Assizes (the high court, which tried cases for which capital punishment was a possible sentence).[31]

Most assaults were by men against men. A few were by women against women. Very few were by men against women.[32]

The minutes of the Quarter Sessions for the London District record one case in which it appears that an entire family was charged with assault and battery in 1818. The Best family first appears in the records on 16 May, when the court ordered a bench warrant issued for John Best, John's wife, and John's son, Cosper Best, requiring them to appear at the next Quarter Sessions to answer charges. On 14 July, John Best, Mrs. Best, and Cosper Best appeared, as required, but were told to return the next day and given permission to go home.

There is no record of the Best family on the 15th, but on the 16th they appeared again. This time there were four of them: John, Dota (presumably John's wife), Cosper, and Ann. Each were required to put up £100 to assure their appearance at the *next* Quarter Sessions. John Young and Philip Young were also required to put up £50 each for each of member of the Best family, as their sureties. There's a note that says all the court costs were paid up to that date.

On 13 October, the Best family finally began their trial. John, Dota, Cosper, and Ann were all present, a jury of twelve men was sworn in. Caleb ? [Wood, I think] and Jeremiah Young were also sworn in as witnesses. Then there is a note, "Prisoner Ann Best not Guilty," and the court was adjourned until the next day.

On the 14th, John Best, Dota Best, and Cosper Best were arraigned again and plead not guilty. Another jury of twelve men (only five of whom were on the previous day's jury) was sworn in, Caleb Wood, Joseph Kitchen, and Matthew Tisdale were sworn in as witnesses for the prosecution; Jeremiah Young and Ann Best were sworn in as witnesses for the defence. The jury found the prisoners guilty. John Best was fined £1 10s.; Mrs Best was fined 15s. and Cosper Best was fined 5s. They were ordered to be imprisoned until they paid their fines, but they paid them promptly to the sheriff. [33]

It should be noted that even the most prominent citizens appeared in the Quarter Session records convicted of assault. It didn't seem to affect their reputations or success in life.[34]

More serious crimes were another matter. Between 1827 and 1846 there were twenty cases of murder brought before the Niagara District Assizes. In seven cases, the accused were convicted, in ten cases they were acquitted, two cases weren't heard, and one of the accused was judged insane and therefore unable to stand trial. Of the twenty accused, three were women. Of these, two were acquitted and one was found guilty of a lesser charge (concealing the birth of a child).[35]

Only eight cases of rape were brought before the Niagara Assizes in the same period (as rape was a capital offence, it was not eligible to be tried at the Quarter Sessions). Six of the eight were acquitted. Very likely the low number of cases is due to the low conviction rate. The conviction rate rose dramatically after 1842, when legislation allowed conviction for "assault with intent to rape."[36]

In some cases, magistrates decided to prosecute for assault instead of rape. This allowed them to take the case to the Quarter Sessions (which was less intimidating and quicker) instead of the Assizes, and to increase the likelihood of conviction.

For example, in October 1836, Samuel Hathaway Farensworth of St. Catharines, yeoman, was charged with "assault with intent to carnally know a child under ten years of age." The victim was a seven-year-old girl who had been living with Farensworth for a few weeks in the summer. The girl's father prosecuted the case, bringing fourteen witnesses, including three doctors. The doctors all agreed that the child had been assaulted, which appears to have been rare. In all, twenty-nine witnesses and three constables testified at the lengthy trial. The jury convicted Farensworth and he received a sentence of three months in gaol and a fine of £25 and court costs, which would have been in the order of £20 (the fine would be equivalent to about seventy days work for a skilled labourer, perhaps $13,000

R. vs. Samuel Farensworth, Cover Page of Bill of Indictment, October 1836, Lincoln County Court of General Quarter Sessions of the Peace Records, Archives of Ontario, RG 22-372 Box 25 Folder 22.

now[37]). He complained bitterly about the costs, saying that several of the witnesses were either not necessary or didn't need to attend court for more than one day (witnesses were paid 2s. 6d. per day in court, plus mileage).[38]

Age was a significant factor, as carnal knowledge of a girl under ten was a capital offence (punishable by execution),[39] while carnal knowledge of a girl over ten but under twelve was still considered a misdemeanor.[40]

There were very few prosecutions for wife beating. Women almost never asked for the protection of the law unless they believed their lives were threatened. Even then, there were few convictions for assault, mostly because the wives wouldn't prosecute or no witness could be found. Instead, the magistrates resorted to the use of peace bonds. A single magistrate could require a man to sign a recognizance (legal obligation to pay a certain amount to the Crown) on condition of keeping the peace with his wife (or whoever the victim was) for a period of time, usually one year, and to find two sureties who would sign with him. A typical recognizance for keeping the peace was £50, with each of the sureties bound for half that amount.[41]

Crimes Against Property

Crimes against property were the most common offences tried at the Assizes. This includes such offences as theft, larceny, stealing, burglary, destruction of property, receiving stolen property, and fraud. Theft and larceny were the most common.[43] Between 1828 and 1841 in the Niagara District, there were 234 prosecutions for larceny at the Quarter Sessions and 77 at the Assizes.[44] According to the Gore District gaol records, between 1832 and 1840, the average rate of crimes against property was 107 per 100,000.[45]

Crimes Against Property Prosecuted
in the Niagara District[42]

	Larceny Quarter Sessions	Larceny at Assizes
1828	6	6
1829	14	2
1830	18	6
1831	16	5
1832	10	3
1833	17	2
1834	15	5
1835	20	8
1836	17	4
1837	36	6
1838	10	11
1839	16	7
1840	29	5
1841	10	7

Before 1789, petty larceny was defined as larceny of up to 1s.; grand larceny was larceny over 1s. As grand larceny was a capital offence (i.e., punishable by death), an Ordinance of 1789[46] raised the limit for petty larceny to 20s. in order to keep small thefts from clogging the high courts. Grand larceny was over 20s.

Anyone committed to gaol for petty larceny had to find bail within forty-eight hours (so he could be released on his recognizance to wait for trial at the Quarter Sessions), otherwise three Justices of the Peace could convict of petty larceny in petty sessions (without a jury).[47] In the 1820s grand larceny often brought six months in gaol and thirty-nine lashes.[48] The distinction between grand and petty larceny was removed in 1837.[49]

Crimes Against the Moral Order

Moral offences included abusive language, breach of by-laws, drunk and disorderly conduct, gambling, public nuisance, keeping a disorderly house, and vagrancy. In the Gore District between 1832 and 1840, the average rate of crimes against public order was thirty-three per 100,000.[50]

As the districts were very autonomous in the early days, each had its own approach to dealing with moral order offences. In some districts, such as Newcastle, very few such crimes appear in the records, in others, such as London, the authorities were more vigilant. For example, between 1800 and 1820 there were four cases of profane swearing. All were convicted, and sentences ranged from fines of 2s. to 6s. Three men were fined 3s. 4d. each for breaking the Sabbath.[51] In the Gore District, drunk and disorderly was by far the most common moral offence.[52] Moral order crimes represented 12 to 13 percent of the total arrests in the Niagara District.[53]

In one case reported in Toronto's *Colonial Advocate* in 1834, a woman named Ellen Halfpenny appeared in Police Court for the third time in six weeks, charged with being drunk and disorderly. After having sentenced her to brief gaol stays the first two instances (just a few days), the third time the police report reads: "Ellen Halfpenny, a common scold, drunken and disorderly, set in the stocks and ordered to clean prison cells."[54]

Regulatory Offences

Regulatory offences included such things as selling liquor without a licence or refusing to perform statute labour. These generally brought summary convictions (i.e., they didn't require a jury trial). Magistrates weren't required to record their summary convictions before 1834, so there are few records of these.[55]

A newspaper report of the Toronto Police Court activities for early June 1834, recorded two regulatory offences: James Sloan of New Street was fined £20 for selling spirituous liquors without a licence; and Wellington G. Armstrong was fined 6s. and 3d. for refusing to assist a constable in the execution of his duty.[56]

Political Crimes

Upper Canada cases suggest that the administration of criminal law was repressive, even by contemporary British standards of constitutionalism and legality.[57] Sedition proceedings were used to suppress political dissent several times between 1804 and 1828, including proceedings against Joseph Willcocks, the editor of the province's first firmly established independent newspapers, Robert Gourlay, and Francis Collins another newspaper editor.[58]

Francis Collins began his newspaper career as a compositor for the King's printer, the *Upper Canada Gazette*. By early 1821, he was reporting on the debates in the House of Assembly, providing much more information than any newspaper had previously. However, he sympathized with the reform cause and gave more coverage to the reformers' point of view than to the Tories. For that, he aroused the ire of the establishment. When the publisher of the *Gazette* retired late in 1821, Collins hoped to take over, but was refused because he was not "a gentleman." In July 1825 he founded his own newspaper, the *Canadian Freeman*, which he used to attack the government and its Tory connections. In 1828 he was charged with four counts of libel. When the judge allowed him to make a statement in court (having appeared without counsel), he took the opportunity to attack the Attorney

General (who was prosecuting Collins' case) for dereliction of duty in not prosecuting the rioters who had destroyed William Lyon Mackenzie's press a couple of years previously. Three of the four charges were withdrawn and he was acquitted of the fourth, but the Attorney General then laid two new charges: one for a libel on himself and the other for a disrespectful reference to a judge. The jury convicted Collins on the first charge and the judge sentenced Collins to one year in gaol, a fine of £50, and sureties of £600 for good behaviour for three years — a sentence widely condemned as out of all proportion to the offence.[59]

Records Relating to Criminal Law

For British law (which applied in Upper Canada unless explicitly revoked by an Upper Canadian statute), your best source is Blackstone's Commentaries:

Blackstone, Sir William. *Commentaries on the Laws of England*, 4 Volumes, First Edition. Oxford: Clarendon Press, 1765–1769. This is available online in several places, my preference being: *avalon.law.yale.edu/subject_menus/blackstone.asp*

For Upper Canadian law (modifications to British law) see:

The Statutes of the Province of Upper Canada [1792–1831]: Together With Such British Statutes, Ordinances of Quebec, and Proclamations, as Relate to the Said Province. Revised and printed for, and published by Hugh C. Thomson and James Macfarlane. Revised by James Nickalls, Jr. Kingston: Printed by Francis M. Hill, 1831 (privately printed, but taking the place of an authorized publication).

The Statutes of Upper Canada, to the Time of the Union. Revised and published by authority. Toronto: Robert Stanton, Printer to the Queen's Most Excellent Majesty, [c. 1843].

Harrison, Robert A. *A Digest of Reports of all Cases Determined in the Queen's Bench and Practice Courts for Upper Canada from 1823 to 1851 Inclusive* [microform]: *Being From the Commencement of Taylor's Reports to the End of Vol. VII Upper Canada Reports, [Cameron's digests included]: With an Appendix Containing the Digests of Cases Reported in Vol. VIII Upper Canada reports 1852.* H. Rowsell (Canadian Institute of Historical Microreproductions (CIHM), fiche 10817).

For municipal laws, see the minutes of council and published by-laws of the relevant town/city, usually held in local archives.

CHAPTER TWO

Law Enforcement and Investigation

Law Enforcement

For most of the Upper Canada period, law enforcement was primitive. The population was sparse and there was neither a need, nor sufficient funds for a professional police force. As was the case in eighteenth-century England, the role of keeping the peace and enforcing the law fell upon local magistrates. See Chapter Six for a full discussion of the role of magistrates.[1]

From its founding, Upper Canada was divided into administrative districts, and each district operated with a great deal of autonomy. In 1788 there were four districts. As the population grew new districts were created. By 1841, there were twenty.[2] Each district had a Clerk of the Peace, a sheriff, and several magistrates.

Magistrates (formally known as Justices of the Peace) had both administrative and judicial functions. They were, in effect, the local (district or county) government. They set tax rates, appointed local officials, paid salaries, enforced local regulations, held court, and generally maintained public order.[3]

The magistrates were assisted in these duties by the sher-iff[4] and civilian part-time constables[5] appointed for duty on an annual basis (see Chapter Six for a full discussion of the roles of the magistrate, sheriff, and constable). Other than inspecting roads, bridges, and chimneys for safety purposes, the sheriff and his constables did not actively go looking for criminal activity, as we expect our police to do now. The sheriff's job was to enforce the will of the court by summoning jurors for jury duty, making arrests, looking after the gaol, and maintaining order in the courthouse.[6] Constables followed orders received from magistrates, generally including executing search warrants, making arrests, delivering prisoners to gaol or court, and serving subpoenas on witnesses.[7]

Expenses for the administration of justice were covered by taxes and fines. For example, the inhabitants of the Town of York were divided into income classes for taxes. In 1798 there were 112 taxpayers in ten classes. The lowest class paid 1s. 3d. per year (twenty-six people), the highest class paid 18s. 6d. (three people).[8]

Investigation

Most minor crimes were probably never reported due to the inconvenience involved and the fact that many Christian communities, especially evangelical denominations, forbade their members from using secular courts to settle conflicts between members. They were supposed to try to work it out between themselves, and if that failed get help from the church. In the case of Presbyterians, the minister and church elders were in charge of disciplining members. In Baptist churches all church members shared the responsibility to oversee each others' behaviour and to help settle disputes. We do not know as much about Methodist disciplinary procedures, as they didn't keep records of their disciplinary proceedings.[9]

Lynn Marks' study of church disciplinary records provides the following example:

> The records of Norwich Baptist church include a
> lengthy discussion of the case of William G., who
> was accused of treating his wife very badly. Both
> his wife and two witnesses testified that he had
> spoken very abusively to her. Mrs H., who lived
> in the same house as the Gs, stated that "when
> she went into their room Mr G. would appear
> to be very pleasant to his wife, but witness saith
> that Mr G. did nights after he had got to bed
> scold his wife and threaten her, saying he could
> break her bones and he should be justified in so
> doing." As a result of G's "hard threats and tyran-
> nical behaviour to [his] wife," as well as his refusal
> to support her any longer, and his further refusal
> to come before the church to answer charges on
> these matters, the Norwich church "withdrew
> [their] Christian hand of fellowship" from him.[10]

The criminal justice process generally began with the victim bringing attention to the crime by making a report.[11] This involved travelling to the nearest magistrate to file an "information": a signed statement containing all of the information the person could provide concerning the offence. In the very early days, this might mean travelling one hundred miles or more [160 km]. As time progressed, magistrates were appointed throughout the districts, so that in theory, everyone had easy access (at least one within each township by the 1830s).

Information of Carson Mosier, 11 January 1835, Criminal Case Files, Western District Court of General Quarter Sessions of the Peace, Archives of Ontario, RG 22-110.

If the accusation involved a suspicious death or fire, the coroner would launch an investigation (assuming there was a coroner available, if there wasn't the magistrate would perform his role).[12] The coroner had authority to summon and hear testimony from witnesses, call on medical personnel for their opinions, and gather whatever other evidence he required. He could then call a coroner's jury[13] to examine the evidence and make a verdict concerning the cause of death or the cause of the fire. Most of the evidence

Western District   }   An inquisition indented, taken for our Sovereign Lord
     to wit   the King at the Township of Sombra in the County of Kent
in the Western District the thirtieth day of May in the sixth
year of the reign of Our Sovereign Lord William the fourth &c. before Peter
Paul Lacroix, Esquire one of the Coroners of Our said Lord the King for
the said District on view of the body of William Henry Cooke then and
there lying dead upon the oath of James Leys, James Stewart Sr, James
Stewart Junr, John Stewart, Laughlin McDonald, Hugh McDonald,
John McDonald, Daniel McDonald, Mathew Little, James Fisher,
A. A. Brentnell, John (Taylor) McDonald and Hiram Brentnell good
and lawful men of the said Township duly chosen and who being there
and there duly sworn and charged to inquire for Our said Lord the King
when, where how and after what manner the said William Henry Cooke
came to his death, do, upon their oath say that the said William Henry
Cooke, on the seventeenth day of May instant in a certain river called the
north branch of Bearcreek at the Township and in the County and District
aforesaid, accidentally, casually and by misfortune was in the waters of the
said river then and there suffocated and drowned of which said suffocation
and drowning he the said William Henry Cooke then and there instantly
died, And so the said Jurors upon their oath aforesaid, do, say, that the
said William Henry Cooke in the manner aforesaid having no marks of
violence appearing on his body departed this life by the visitation of God.
In witness whereof as well the said Coroner as the Jurors aforesaid have
to this inquisition set their hands and seals on the day and year and at the
place first above mentioned.

P.P. Lacroix Coroner —   John J. McDonald

James Leys   Donald McDonald

James Stewart   Matthew Little

James Stewart Junr   James Fisher

John Stewart   Asa Brentnell

Laughlin McDonald   John McDonald

Hugh McDonald   Hiram Brentnell

Inquisition on the body of William Henry Cooke, 13 May 1836, Coroner's
Records, Western District Court of General Quarter Sessions of the Peace, Archives
of Ontario, RG 22-1826.

Warrant of arrest for Charles Ragan on charge of larceny, 11 January 1835, Criminal Case Files, Western District Court of General Quarter Sessions of the Peace, Archives of Ontario, RG 22-110.

was gathered by examining witnesses and recording their statements, usually called affidavits or depositions. See Chapter Six for a full discussion of the role of the coroner and the coroner's jury.

If the crime did not involve a suspicious death or fire, responsibility for the investigation would fall on the local Justice of the Peace with the assistance of the sheriff and his constables. Professional police forces began to appear in the late 1830s.

For relatively minor matters, the magistrate would issue a summons for the suspect to appear before him, or before the relevant court on a certain date. For more serious crimes, he would issue a warrant for the arrest of the suspect. The warrant would then be given to a constable with instructions to locate the suspect, place him or her under arrest, and deliver him or her to the district or county gaol.

Making an arrest could sometimes be difficult, even hazardous. Constables had no special training, were unarmed, and often had to travel great distances in rotten weather to locate and apprehend a suspect. In the Newcastle District alone there were at least fifty incidents (likely many more that weren't prosecuted) in which constables or bailiffs were assaulted or threatened between 1813 and 1840.[14]

> When William Wadsworth, a Queenston constable, threatened Barney Woolman with a prosecution while a card game was going on in a local tavern, Woolman punched him in the mouth, loosening a tooth. "As you are going to take the Law of me," he said, "I will give you something to take the Law for." Woolman pleaded guilty to assault and battery and received a token fine of one shilling and costs.[15]

Recognizance of Joseph Willcox, Bail Book of William Dummer Powell, unbound papers, 1803, Baldwin Room, Toronto Public Library, L16.

Here you see the style of cause, "King vs. Joseph Willcox," the charge "libel," the name of the defendant, Joseph Willcox, the amount of his recognizance, "£200," the names of his two sureties, Benjamin Davis and Joseph Sheppard, both of the Township of York, Husbandmen, and the amount of their recognizances, "£100" each. Finally, you see the conditions of the recognizance: the appearance of Joseph Willcox on the first day of the next term, being Hilary 48th Geo. 3rd (Hilary's term is January to March, the 48th year of King George III's reign, which was 1808), to the Court of King's Bench at York and to attend every day until discharged by the court.

However, despite the danger and low pay, it would appear that most constables carried out their orders very well, receiving praise from the magistrates. Frances Ann Thompson's study of the Niagara District records revealed that there were very few complaints about the conduct of constables.[16]

Most of the time, once a suspect was arrested he stayed in gaol until the next session of the court. Towards the end of the Upper Canada period it became more common for the accused to swear out a recognizance (along with two of his supporters), which would allow him to be released temporarily pending trial. If he didn't appear, he and his sureties would owe the court the amount of the recognizance — usually a very large amount.

Investigative Records

Investigative records are generally filed under the name of the clerk who created and maintained the records (Clerk of the Peace, criminal Assize clerk, etc.) or the relevant level of court (Quarter Sessions, Assizes).

Note: This inventory only contains records that begin before 1841. Many other records will be available for the post-1841 period. See Abbreviations Used for a list of repository abbreviations.

Case Files or Filings

Case files or filings contain a wide range of documents prepared in the course of the investigation and trial. They can include: recognizances, summonses, warrants, informations, examinations, indictments, police reports, exhibits such as maps or photographs, coroner's records, and lists of evidence.

Inventory

Assize Records

- AO RG 4-1, Boxes 6–7 Crown Prosecutions Case files, 1799–1843.
- AO RG 22-138 Court of King's Bench Criminal Assize Filings, 1792–1799, 1815–1819. These are all indexed in the ADD by defendant's name, a total of twenty-seven cases, plus a file of recognizances for the Eastern District, 1798/1799.
- TPL L16 William Dummer Powell papers, B85: bound book "Circuit Papers" 1788–1820. Includes miscellaneous papers relating to a wide range of cases, including affidavits, a coroner's inquest and indictment, an information, a jury summons, and several petitions.

Quarter Sessions Records

- AO RG 22-14 Johnstown District (Brockville), Court of General Quarter Sessions of Peace case files, 1802–1846.
- AO RG 22-32 Newcastle District (Cobourg) Court of General Quarter Sessions of the Peace filings, 1803–1848. There are no records for 1845 or 1847.
- AO RG 22-96 York County (York/Toronto) Court of General Sessions of the Peace filings. There are only a smattering of documents for the years 1796–1799, 1828, 1832, and 1838.
- AO RG 22-109 Western District (Windsor) Court of General Quarter Sessions of Peace case files, 1821–1859 in Hiram Walker Collection, MS 205.
- AO RG 22-110 Western District (Windsor) Court of General Quarter Sessions of Peace filings, 1822–1859 in Hiram Walker Collection, MS 205.

- AO RG 22-372 Lincoln County/Niagara District (St. Catharines) Court of General Quarter Sessions of Peace filings, 1828–1919.
- TUA 90-005 Victoria County fonds, 1834–1969: General Quarter Sessions of the Peace records.
- TUA United Counties of Northumberland and Durham. Court records fonds, 1803–1955: includes General Quarter Sessions of the Peace filings.

Coroner's Investigation or Inquest Records

Coroner's records usually contain only the final report written by the coroner's jury. However, in some cases you will also find records of their investigation, such as summons and examinations. The final report will describe the findings of the jury (i.e., how the deceased met his death and whether it should be classed as a criminal offence, accident, or natural causes), and recommendations for actions to be taken to avoid similar events in the future. The report is signed by all the jurors.

Records of coroner's inquests and investigations may be found in local county or district archives and also at the Archives of Ontario. They may be embedded in records of the quarter sessions, so check files and filings records, as well as those labelled "coroner's" records.

Inventory

- AO RG 22-1826 Western District Court of General Quarter Sessions of Peace, coroner's investigations and inquests, 1835–1836.
- AO RG 22-3195 Lincoln County/Niagara District,

Court of General Quarter Sessions of Peace, coroner's investigations and inquests, 1834–1917.

- AO RG 22-3395 Middlesex County/London District, Court of General Quarter Sessions of Peace, coroner's investigations and inquests, 1831–1893.
- AO RG 22-3788 Newcastle District, Court of General Quarter Sessions of Peace, coroner's investigations and inquests, 1821–1848.
- AO GS microfilm, Huron County, Court of General Quarter Sessions of Peace, coroner's records, 1841–1904.
- AO GS microfilm Middlesex County/London District, Court of General Quarter Sessions of Peace, coroner's records, 1831–1835.
- TUA 90-005 Victoria County fonds, 1834–1969: General Quarter Sessions of the Peace, includes Inquests.
- TUA United Counties of Northumberland and Durham, Index to Coroner's Inquests:
- *www.trentu.ca/admin/library/archives/84-020%20inquestucnd.htm.* HCM Coroner's Inquest — December 8th, 1841.

Police Records

Police records can include a wide range of records including personnel records, day books, arrest warrants and registers, bail books, correspondence, and financial records. They can be found in municipal archives and in private police archives. Professional police forces did not develop until after the Upper Canada period, so there are no specific records for them prior to 1841.

The earliest records for the Toronto City Police, the first professional police force in Ontario, begin in 1849. They are housed at the City of Toronto Archives.

Private Papers

Records pertaining to criminal investigations may sometimes be found in private papers, particularly of justice personnel. This inventory cannot hope to be complete, but provides a starting point for researchers.

Inventory

High Court Judges
TPL L16 William Dummer Powell papers:

- B85: bound book "Circuit Papers" 1788–1820. Includes miscellaneous papers relating to a wide range of cases, including affidavits, a coroner's inquest and indictment, an information, a jury summons, and several petitions.
- B87: Papers regarding prisoners and trials throughout Upper Canada, 1794–1825. Mostly calendars of prisoners, also a few jury lists.

Justices of the Peace
- LAC R3800-0-3-E (formerly MG24 D108) Robert Nelles fonds 1782–1848. Series consists of chronologically arranged papers of Robert Nelles and his family. The reports and affidavits largely pertain to his career and activities as a Member of Legislative Assembly and a Justice of the Peace respectively.
- NHS Records of Justice of the Peace, Francis Leigh Walsh (1824–1880).
- TPL S113 Alexander Wood papers, 1798–1837. Correspondence and court filings while Justice of the Peace in York, 180 pieces.

• TUA 71-006 John Huston fonds, 1818–1849. Includes his papers as Justice of the Peace.

Clerks of the Peace

• LAC MG9 D8-14 Johnstown District collection: the papers of Edward Jessup, Clerk of the Peace 1800–1801, 102 pages. Series consists of papers preserved by Edward Jessup while Clerk of the Peace. Included are two pages and miscellaneous papers relating to prosecutions before the Court of General Quarter Sessions of the Peace for the Johnstown District. A list of individuals involved precedes the volumes.

• NHS Thomas Welch Papers, Clerk of the Court, London District. Court Papers, 1796–1816.

• PCMA Peterborough County Court fonds, 1830–1909. Clerk of the Peace Records, Criminal Court Cases, indictments.

Sheriffs

• LAC R4024-0-6-E (formerly MG24 I26 volumes 44–48) Alexander Hamilton and family fonds, records of the sheriff and various courts of the Niagara District, 1818–1837.

• LAC R6180-0-5-E (formerly MG24 I27) John McEwan fonds, 1811–1868. Fonds consists of correspondence and papers of Captain John McEwan including some legal documents acquired while he was sheriff of Essex County.

• LAC R4029-0-2-E (formerly MG24 I8) MacDonell Family Fonds, Allan MacDonell papers, 1837–1868. Series consists of papers and records collected as sheriff of Gore, 1837–1843 relating primarily to the Rebellion of 1837.

- LAC R3944-0-4-E (formerly MG24 I73) J. W. Dunbar Moodie fonds. Official correspondence received by Moodie while he was sheriff of the Victoria District 1839–1863.
- TUA 90-005 Victoria County fonds, 1834–1969: General Quarter Sessions of the Peace, includes sheriff's books.

Correspondence and Miscellaneous Records

Inventory

- AO RG 22-119 Western District (Windsor) Court of General Quarter Sessions of Peace, correspondence, 1792–1881 in Hiram Walker Collection, MS 205.
- AO RG 22-120 Western District (Windsor) Court of General Quarter Sessions of Peace, miscellaneous, 1808–1853 in Hiram Walker Collection, MS 205.
- BULA McEwen, Ann Alexandra. *Crime in the Niagara District, 1827–1850.* Guelph: University of Guelph, Dept. of History, 1991. Unpublished Thesis.
- BULA Thompson, Frances Ann. *Local Authority and District Autonomy: The Niagara Magistracy and Constabulary, 1828–1841.* Ottawa: University of Ottawa, 1996. Unpublished Thesis.

Treason and Rebellion Investigations

Many of the informations (testimony) relating to treason during the War of 1812 and the Rebellion of 1837 can be found in the Upper Canada Sundries (LAC RG 5 A1 Correspondence of the Civil Secretary). There is a typed calendar to these records that includes the names of all individuals mentioned in them. It is prepared in chronological order, not alphabetically. A partial alphabetical index (up to 1816), can be found on the author's website: *www.uppercanadagenealogy.com*.

Records of investigations for treason and rebellion are often found separated from regular criminal records. Known collections are as follows.

Inventory

- AO RG22-143: Court of King's Bench records of high treason trial of 1814. Series consists of the few remaining records of the High Treason Trials held at Ancaster during May and June 1814. Included are the following documents: dockets regarding the outlawry of Matthias Brown and Benajah Mallory; two depositions against Eliazir Daggett, Oliver Gran, and Eliakim Crosby; and the indictment against Luther McNeal and an exemplification of judgement against McNeal. Also included with this series are the commissions and inquisitions regarding lands forfeited by those convicted of high treason. The commissions were issued in December 1817, and the inquisitions were held in January 1818. There is also a commission and inquisition for Samuel Thompson dated 1824.
- LAC RG5 B39 Civil Secretary, records relating to Rebellions. Upper Canada. Records of the inquiry into the conduct of Colonel John Prince at the Battle of Windsor, 1839.
- LAC RG5 B43 Civil Secretary, records relating to Rebellions. Upper Canada. Documents relating to the

prosecution of Alexander McLeod for the destruction of the *Caroline*, 1841.

- LAC R4029-0-2-E (formerly MG24 I8) MacDonell Family Fonds, Allan MacDonell papers, 1837–1868. Series consists of papers and records collected as sheriff of Gore, 1837–1843 relating primarily to the Rebellion of 1837.

CHAPTER THREE

Adjudication

A person accused of a crime in Upper Canada was presumed innocent until proven guilty. This was true regardless of the type or severity of the offence. However, there were different types of adjudication. Very minor offences, often called regulatory offences or by-law infractions, such as failing to perform statute labour, being drunk and disorderly, and prostitution, did not require the attention of a court and could be dealt with "summarily" (i.e., without trial by jury) by one or two magistrates. Minor crimes that were not punishable by capital punishment or penitentiary terms were tried at the lower-level criminal courts, called Quarter Sessions. Capital crimes were tried only by the high court, popularly called the Assizes.

Summary Justice

Before 1834, certain minor infractions could be handled informally by local magistrates. A long history of statutes (based on English law, and continuing with Quebec laws prior to the founding of Upper Canada in 1791), stipulated which offences could be decided by a single magistrate, which ones required two magistrates, which required three magistrates, and which had to go before the courts. When two or three magistrates sat together outside the courts, their sessions were called "Petty Sessions." Those sessions did not require a jury. This was called "Summary Justice."[1]

After 1834, magistrates gained a great deal of authority, so a single Justice of the Peace could hear a wide range of minor cases without a jury. These included simple assault, willful or malicious damage to real or personal property, and willful disturbance of a religious congregation by rude and indecent behaviour or noise.[2]

The 1833 Act to Provide for the Summary Punishment of Petty Trespasses and Other Offences, 4 William IV (1834), c.4 also laid down formal regulations for how summary prosecutions were handled. First, the prosecution had to take place within three months of the alleged offence. The accused had to be summoned to appear by a Justice of the Peace. If the accused didn't appear, the magistrate could proceed without his or her presence (*ex parte*). He summoned witnesses, heard all the evidence, and then discharged or levied a fine, forfeiture, or penalty up to £5. He could also decide to refer the case to the Court of Quarter Sessions and commit the accused for trial with or without bail.[3]

If there was a conviction, but either the accused or the prosecutor (generally the victim) felt that justice had not been served, he or she could appeal to next general Quarter Session, giving notice to the other party in writing within three days of summary conviction and seven days before the session.[4]

The legislative change also required magistrates to register their summary convictions with the next Quarter Sessions, including the records of money gathered from fines, forfeitures, or penalties. As a result, we have a great deal more evidence of their activities for the later period.[5]

Another set of regulations required Justices of the Peace who wanted to send a case to trial at the Quarter Sessions to take down the complainant's testimony in writing, show it to the accused, and let him or her cross-examine the complainant. The magistrates could then determine if bail should be granted. One magistrate could commit the accused to jail if there was "positive and credible evidence of a felony having been committed" but it required two magistrates to determine bail.[6]

Many magistrates also likely helped people settle disputes without formal charges, sometimes using formal arbitration bonds or other legal documents.[7] Indeed, this seems to have been encouraged. Attorney General Henry Boulton replied to a question about the amount of discretion available to magistrates in 1830, saying, "Magistrates may exercise their discretion in allowing persons to compromise trifling misdemeanours where the interest of the public do not require an example to be made … by discouraging the prosecution of petty offences not affecting the public, I conceive they will best discharge their duty and serve the public interests."[8]

Also, many offences that ought to have been considered serious and go before the Quarter Sessions or Assizes were actually given lesser charges and tried summarily by Justices of the Peace. This was done to avoid disrupting community relations and because it was quicker and more convenient. Both victims and magistrates had a great deal of discretion in deciding how to pursue a case.[9]

Police Villages and Boards of Police

As villages and towns got larger some acquired police powers, which meant some degree of additional jurisdiction, such as to enact by-laws concerning local safety issues (mostly for fire prevention) and

City Police Report.

James Sloan of New Street, on the evidence of Charles Callaghan, &c. convicted of selling spirituous Liquors without License and fined £20.

June 4th.—John Davis (a man of colour) Labourer, convicted on the evidence of Thomas Johnson, and others of being riotous and disorderly, and of beating biting and violently assaulting said Johnson—sentenced to 14 days confinement and to be employed breaking stones.

James Lavins, formerly a school master in Markham, on the evidence of the High Bailiff and others —sentenced to be confined 7 days, with hard labour, for being found drunk in the public streets, and creating a disturbance. This was his second offence within the week.

Thomas Cooper sentenced to three days Imprisonment for being riotous and disorderly in the Streets when drunk—On the complaint of the High Bailiff.

June 5.—Edward Harrington a Private in the 15th Regiment brought up on a charge of Drunkenness.—discharged after being admonished.

George A. Barber, Esquire, U. C. College, preferred a complaint against John Wilson of this City for having a Cow Bell in his possession which (as was alledged) was stolen from him last August. The case dismissed.

City Police Report, the Advocate, *12 June 1834, 3.*

market regulations. Village or town magistrates could convict by-law offenders summarily, imposing small fines as punishment.

In the town of York, for example, a police office was formed in 1826, where a magistrate would be on duty every day to hear and deal with minor complaints. The most common offences were public drunkenness, disorderly conduct, and selling spirits without a licence. The summary jurisdiction of the police office continued, even after Toronto became a city with its own Mayor's Court, even though the mayor automatically became the police office magistrate as well as presiding over the Mayor's Court (see page 64). Unfortunately, there was no requirement to keep records of summary convictions made by the police magistrates, so no known official records have survived. Our main sources of information about the Police Court are newspaper reports.[10]

Incorporated towns acquired elected governing structures, called boards of police, headed by a mayor. Within the town limits, the board of police had special jurisdiction to decide minor cases without a jury. In addition to the members of the board, the only people who attended the court were a bailiff or constable, the prosecutor/victim, defendant, and witnesses brought by them.[11] The first town to become incorporated in Upper Canada was Brockville in 1832. Other towns soon followed, including Hamilton in 1833; Belleville, Cornwall, Port Hope, and Prescott in 1834; Cobourg and Picton in 1837.[12] More extensive powers were granted to cities and towns incorporated by special acts of legislation: Toronto (city) in 1834, Kingston (town) in 1838.[13]

Based on the records of the Prescott board of police, it seems that in the early years the poor and working class residents of towns made ample use of this low-level court to air disputes with their neighbours. Women were frequently represented in the records as both plaintiffs/prosecutors and defendants, even married women, who in theory were not supposed to act as independent persons under the law. In fact, the minutes even record one case of a married woman successfully prosecuting her husband for disturbing the peace by striking her.[14] The board of police was less expensive and met far more frequently than the Quarter Sessions, so justice was both accessible and swift. It seems, however, that because of this very openness, townspeople of "means" did not avail themselves of this avenue of justice.[15]

To be eligible to serve on the board of police, a man had to own property of assessed value of at least £60. That meant most board members were merchants or manufacturers. They were elected by male residents who were British subjects and owned a dwelling house and a plot of land or who paid rent of at least £5 a year.[16]

In her study of the Prescott Board of Police records, McKenna found what appeared to be almost verbatim transcripts of the testimony heard before the court, including many examples of verbal insults exchanged by quarrelling women of the town. For example, Catherine Kelleaugher, neighbour of Mary Greneau, who was accused of running a "disorderly house," reported that one evening two women, Bridget Savage and Margaret Doneghan, engaged in a shouting match on the street outside Mary Greneau's house, calling each other "bitch," "whore," and "bastard."[17]

Convictions by police magistrates and board of police could be appealed to the Quarter Sessions of the district, similar to summary convictions by district magistrates.

Pre-Trial Events

If the case had to go to court the first step was for the magistrate to forward the evidence he had gathered to the Clerk of the Peace for record keeping. The magistrate then decided whether to take the case to the Quarter Sessions or the Assizes. Often, a serious case would first go to the Quarter Sessions where all the magistrates could jointly decide whether it needed to be moved to the higher court. The magistrate then selected the necessary witnesses, and prepared summonses and sent them to the sheriff to be served.

The sheriff assigned the summons to whichever constable was available for the township where the witness lived and the constable delivered it. This had to be done well before the

Grand jury summons to Thomas Carfrae, Home District Assize, Spring 1835, Ephemera Collection, Baldwin Room, Toronto Public Library.

scheduled date of the trial, so the witnesses could prepare to attend. In some cases, witnesses (even victims who were prosecuting) were required to sign recognizances to guarantee that they would appear on court day.

A bill of indictment then had to be prepared describing the offence for which the accused would be tried and summarizing the prosecution's evidence. In cases of murder or manslaughter, the bill of indictment was drawn up by the coroner. In other cases, the bill of indictment was drawn up by two Justices of the Peace.

Shortly before the court was due to sit, the sheriff drew up two lists of eligible jurors, called panels. Each list had to contain the full names and addresses of at least thirty-two and no more than forty-eight residents of the district.[18] Members of the panels were summoned to appear in court on the first day of the session.

Trial Procedures

Just prior to each court session, a grand jury of at least twelve and up to twenty-four men was selected (the actual number varied

Adjudication

from session to session). The presiding judge or magistrate would
read the charge to the jury, summarizing the cases for the session, often commenting on the general state of the district. For
example, at the spring session of the Mayor's Court in Toronto,
Anna Jameson tells us that the mayor took the opportunity of the
charge to the grand jury to complain "of the increase of crime,
and of poverty, wretchedness, and disease ... within the bounds
of the city, and particularly of the increase of street beggars and
juvenile depredators, and he recommends the erection of a house
of industry on a large scale."[19]

William Dummer Powell's charge to the grand jury in
Cornwall, 9 August 1825, reads:

> The charges in the Kalendar [*sic*] for the district
> are limited to one case of rape and two of pey-
> ing. The former a crime of peculiar atrocity in
> as much as it consists of force and violence. To
> the weaker sex universaly [*sic*] admitted to be
> the disgrace and shame of mankind — [illegible
> word - cnclime? evilime?] of the civil violation
> of the law of nature and society. The injury to the
> immediate feelings of the patient and the sort of
> disgrace which is absurdly permitted to attach to
> the innocent sufferer. Juries are called upon by
> consideration for their own security, happiness
> and honor to leave no opportunity for a renewal
> of the offence by the same [illigible word - p???].
> In as much however as this crime is odious in
> itself and obnoxious to society it behoves [*sic*]
> us to be cautious in applying the charge. It is
> of a nature readily to be invented and of dif-
> ficult proof. The evidence is commonly limited

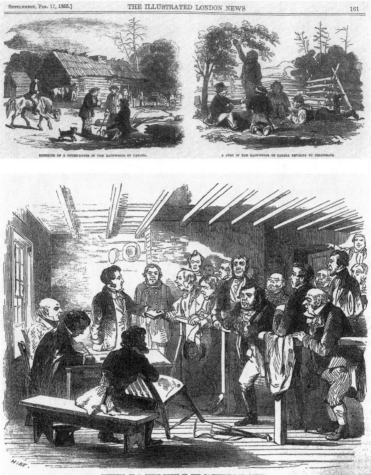

"Exterior of a Court-house in the Backwoods of Canada," "A Jury in the Back-woods of Canada Retiring to Deliberate," and "Interior of a Court-House in the Backwoods of Canada)," Illustrated London News, *Supplement, 17 February 1855, 161.*

to the party making the charge and must generally be supported on her evidence; you cannot
be too careful in ascertaining that the crime has
been committed and that the person of the corp

[illegible word, carried?] has been violated. The
other [two illegible words] evidence of the fact
is of the province of the petty jury, who will
decide upon the evidence of the accumulation
by most minute examination.[20]

Some judges were known for their extremely verbose charges.
Assize judge James B. Macaulay's charges, for example, typically
took up a dozen pages in his notebooks.

After attending to their other duties (such as inspecting the
gaol), the grand jury would meet in a private room separate from
the open court. Not all early courthouses were large enough to
have a separate room, so the grand jury would meet somewhere
else first. The jury was then presented with bills of indictment for
each case in the docket. They considered the evidence provided
by the prosecution and for each case decided whether the Crown
had sufficient evidence for the case to proceed to trial. If twelve
grand jurors agreed, they wrote "true bill." If the grand jury considered the charges groundless, then the indictment was deemed
"not a true bill" or "not found" and the accused was released.[21]

Once the accused was indicted, the case was tried before the
petit jury. A unique group of twelve petit jurors was chosen for
each trial. The *Act for the Regulation of Juries* spelled out the procedure for choosing these juries. The names of the member of the
jury panel were taken from the sheriff's list, written on separate
slips of paper, and put in a box. When the court began, an impartial officer of the court was to draw one name at a time, calling out each name three times, until there were twelve selected.
Sometimes this might require drawing more than twelve names,
as some potential jurors might not have appeared in court (they
would be fined), or might have their impartiality challenged by
either the prosecution or defence.

Bill of Indictment, Barney Woolman, for assault, 1833, Lincoln County Court of General Sessions of the Peace Records, Archives of Ontario, RG 22-372, Box 16, Folder 55.

Most prosecutions were initiated by the victims (or their relatives) of a crime.[22] At the Quarter Sessions, victims gathered their own witnesses and presented their cases in court.[23] If the prosecutor didn't appear, the defendant was released.

It seems that many cases at the Quarter Sessions were dismissed due to the lack of prosecution, as one particularly quarrelsome woman discovered and used to her advantage. Mary Moodey was charged with assault and battery by three different people between October 1801 and October 1805. The first time,

Mary didn't show up on the day of her trial, but she appeared the next day saying she wasn't ready yet and asked for the case to be held over until the next session. The magistrates agreed, requiring her recognizance of £20 (and that of her sureties, Walter Moodey and Daniel Tiers, who pledged £10 each) to be extended to the next session. When the case came up again in January, Esther Dunham, her prosecutor (presumably the victim of the alleged assault) didn't show up, so the case against Mary was dismissed. There's a note in the minutes pointing out that Esther hadn't been bound in recognizance to prosecute, so they couldn't fine her for wasting the court's time. The clerk was probably making a point to the magistrates!

In October 1805, Mary was charged again with assault and battery in two seemingly separate cases: first by Peter Whitney and second by Jane Mitchell. For the case prosecuted by Peter Whitney, Mary again said she was not ready to defend herself and asked for the case to be put off until the next session. The magistrates agreed and bound her on her recognizance of £20 (her sureties John McBride and Adam Everson pledged £10 each). For the case prosecuted by Jane Mitchell the trial went forward. Twelve jurors were sworn in and the prosecution called four witnesses: Jane Mitchell, Peter Whitney, William Jackson, and George Bond. Mary called four witnesses for her defence: James Kendrick, William Washer, Walter Moodey Jun[r] [junior], and Walter Moodey Sen[r] [senior]. The jury brought forth a verdict of not guilty. The first case kept getting put off (by the magistrates this time) until finally it was due to be heard in January 1806. But Peter Whitney didn't show up, so the case against Mary was dismissed again![24]

During the Upper Canada period the prosecution of cases at the Quarter Sessions was not officially supervised by anyone. The victim, or whoever was taking the role of prosecutor, could hire a lawyer, if he or she chose (or more importantly, had the

List of Witnesses, R. vs. Samuel Farensworth, Lincoln County Court of General Sessions of the Peace Records, Archives of Ontario, RG 22-372, Box 25, Folder 22.

funds). If not, the magistrate simply examined the witnesses himself. Local magistrates generally prepared the cases for the Assizes with help from the Clerks of the Peace. If the case concerned a capital offence, the Attorney General or Solicitor General would conduct the actual prosecution.[25]

If the defendant had the means, he could hire an attorney to represent him, but that was rare in the nineteenth century. Generally, only people accused of capital offences hired defence counsel.

Witnesses for the prosecution were heard first, followed by those for the accused. Some of the witnesses might not have any specific information about the events of the crime, but were there to testify to the accused's "character" and life circumstances.[26]

After all the witnesses were called and evidence presented, the judge or magistrate might have made a short speech instructing the jury on their duties. These statements were often full of hyperbole concerning the moral depravity of the offence and commenting on the behaviour of the accused, witnesses, and lawyers. Sometimes the judges explicitly told the jury what verdict they ought to return.[27] The jury then considered the verdict. In most cases all of this took place on the same day. Few nineteenth-century trials took longer than a few hours.

Although the function of the jury was strictly to consider the facts presented to them and decide whether or not the prosecution had proven the guilt of the accused, they often disregarded the evidence when they believed the prosecution was unjust, or if the penalties were too repugnant. Juries were especially reluctant to convict on serious offences at the Assizes (it is generally believed that this was because they felt the legal punishments were too harsh). For example, in Niagara District, of eleven cases of assault on a constable tried between 1837 and 1850, only five resulted in convictions, despite credible witnesses to the assaults.[28]

Following the reading of the verdict by the jury, convicted criminals were taken into custody by the sheriff and his gaoler to await the end of the Quarter Sessions or Assizes (usually a matter of a few days at most), at which time they would be brought back to court to hear the court pronounce the sentences for all the cases in sequence.

Quarter Sessions

Minor offences that were not dealt with by summary justice were tried by the Courts of General Quarter Sessions of the Peace for each District. They were called Quarter Sessions for short because they met four times a year. These courts were presided over by three local Justices of the Peace. During each session, the court travelled throughout the district, sitting for a few days in each major town so that jurors and witnesses wouldn't have to travel great distances.

In addition to trying minor criminal and civil cases, the Court of Quarter Sessions were responsible for a wide range of administrative duties, such as appointing district officials, issuing licences of all kinds, administering the swearing of oaths, authorizing the building and repair of roads and bridges, and attending to social welfare.[29]

R vs. Charles Ragan, 15 January 1835, Minutes, Western District/Essex County Court of General Quarter Sessions of the Peace, Archives of Ontario, RG 22-103, Volume 2.

The trial of Charles Ragan, of Chatham, for larceny is a typical example. The minutes tell us that Charles Ragan was indicted for larceny on 14 January 1835, the case was heard on the following day, six witnesses testified (Francis Drake, John Jones, Almira Akerly, Carson Mosier, Caleb Akerly, and William Spakman), Ragan was found guilty and sentenced to gaol for six months.[30]

The case files provide a great deal more information. First, from the information of Carson Mosier we learn that early on the evening in question, Mr. Jones had given him a half dollar, some silver change, and a few coppers. These had gone missing and he suspected Charles Ragan of stealing them.[31]

In his deposition, William Spackman, Mosier's apprentice, stated that he locked the money drawer and left Charles Ragan in the house while he went out to feed the horses and visit the shoemaker. On his return about an hour later, Mosier asked him if he'd locked the money drawer, and informed him that the money was gone. He also states that some of the money was then found in the possession of Almira Akerley and Caleb Akerley.[32] Almira Akerley's deposition reveals that she said Charles Ragan had paid her a half a dollar in silver.[33]

Finally, Charles Ragan was examined. He stated that he thought he had paid Almira Akerley about a half a dollar in silver but he forgot where he got the money as he was "pretty middling high" after drinking at Mosier's house.[34]

John Jones, Caleb Akerley, Almira Akerley, and William Spackman had all been bound in recognizance to appear to testify at the Quarter Sessions (£5 each).[35]

The bill of indictment charged Ragan with feloniously stealing, taking, and carrying away the goods and chattel of Carson Mosier, including

... one piece of the current silver coin of this province called an American half dollar of the value of two shillings and six pence — one piece of the current copper coin of this province called a "copper" of the value of one half penny — one other piece of current copper coin of this province called "a half penny token" of the value of one half penny — and one other piece of the current copper coin of this province called "piece copper better than paper" of the value of one half penny.[36]

Mayor's Court

When the City of Toronto was incorporated in 1834 a new form of government and judicial jurisdiction was required to deal with its uniquely urban needs (although Toronto's population had not yet reached 10,000, it would expand rapidly). Toronto's act of incorporation provided for an elected council, with the mayor and aldermen becoming Justices of the Peace within the city limits. A Mayor's Court, which operated almost identically to the district Quarter Sessions, was formed. It was presided over by the mayor and at least one alderman, and cases were tried by grand and petit juries with the mayor deciding on sentencing.

The majority of the cases tried in this court were for either larceny or assault and battery, although there were a few other miscellaneous offences seen over the years, such as riot, affray, receiving stolen property, and forcible entry.[37]

Mayor William Lyon Mackenzie's handling of three cases in June 1834 earned him furious criticism. The first case involved participants in a fight during a St. Patrick's Day dinner. A district magistrate and two government clerks were indicted for assault and battery. The magistrate was acquitted, but the clerks were convicted. Mackenzie sentenced them each to a £5 fine and a week in gaol. By contrast, when the brother of a Reform councilman was convicted of the same offence (the jury recommending him to mercy), Mackenzie only fined him 5s. Two weeks later, Mackenzie sentenced a habitually drunken woman to the stocks after she insulted him in court. Mackenzie defended the first heavy fine and imprisonment by saying that men on the public treasury were so well paid that the fine would hardly be noticed. A week in gaol would be more likely to make them think twice about their actions.[38]

Assizes

The most serious offences — murder, manslaughter, larceny, grand larceny, perjury, bigamy, forgery, felony, uttering (putting counterfeit money into circulation), rape, and cattle and horse theft — were handled by the judges of the Court of King's Bench.

Because there was only one Court of King's Bench, but it was hardly practical to have people travelling from all over the province to the Capital, the judges from the Court of King's Bench were commissioned to hold courts in other locations throughout the province. These courts were called Courts of Oyer and Terminer and General Gaol Delivery. The actual Court of King's Bench, which sat only in the capital, generally only decided on issues of law, not fact. So appeals of rules of law went to the Court of King's Bench.

Just to make things more confusing, sessions of the Court of Oyer and Terminer and General Gaol Delivery were called Assizes, so sometimes people referred to the court itself as the

R. vs. Henry Sovereen, Minutes of the London District Assize, 24 August 1819, Archives of Ontario, RG 22-134.

Assize Court. Until 1837 there was only one Assize per year, after 1837, there were two — spring and fall.

Each of the three judges of the Court of King's Bench took one of the three circuits (Eastern, Home, and Western, not to be confused with the districts by the same names). The judge would usually be joined by one or two local Justices of the Peace to assist the judge with their knowledge of the district and its inhabitants.

Within each district, the court travelled from town to town on a set route. For example, in the fall of 1816, the Western circuit of the Court of Oyer and Terminer and General Gaol Delivery started with Sandwich at the end of August, moved to Charlotteville for two days in early September and then to Grantham for five days in October. Across the entire province, eighty-six cases were tried in 1816.

Notices showing where the Assizes would be sitting and when were published in the newspapers and posted in public places so everyone would know the schedule and could plan accordingly. After all, sittings of the court were major public events and many people planned to attend for entertainment. After each circuit, the judge would make a formal report to the Lieutenant-Governor on all the capital cases in which a conviction was brought.[39]

In August 1819, Henry Sovereen was tried at the London Assize for "feloniously maiming a horse." He was found guilty and sentenced to be executed on Saturday the 2nd of October. But due to widespread sympathy for the condemned man, the judge recommended executive clemency, which was granted.

Thirteen years later, Sovereen was convicted at the same court of brutally murdering his wife and seven of his eleven children. The Assize minutes recorded the barest of details, not even listing the witnesses who appeared in court. But the presiding judge's bench books contain almost verbatim transcriptions of the testimony of the nine witnesses who testified for the prosecution. (Although Sovereen was defended by legal counsel, he did not call any witnesses for the defence.)[40]

Although difficult to read due to the speed with which the notes were taken (the handwriting is a challenge, and there are many shortened words), the bench book provides enough detail that we can almost imagine the trial.

Four of the witnesses were neighbours and relatives who testified that Sovereen came to them two hours before daybreak, asking them to help him. He had been attacked by two men with blackened faces and managed to escape, but feared that his family were being murdered. The witnesses gathered up their weapons and followed him back to the house, where they found the bodies of several of Sovereen's children and his wife lying on the ground outside — all but one were dead, one was clearly dying. They picked them all up and took them into the house. An unhurt child was found inside.

Prisoner in Dock Attended By Tipstaves, *by C. W. Jefferys, The Picture Gallery of Canadian History, Volume 2, 243.*

They all testified that Sovereen appeared to be grieving and concerned about getting a doctor to help his injured daughter. They also said Sovereen did not appear to be drunk and they saw no blood on him. However, they also said they didn't know anyone who wished Sovereen or his family any harm and that they searched for the tracks of the attackers leaving the property and could not find them. Also, most of the bodies were cold (suggesting that they had been dead for much longer than it would have taken for Sovereen to run to their house and return to his). A knife belonging to Sovereen's son (one of the dead children) was found embedded in Sovereen's wife's body. And two other weapons (a fro and mallet — shingling instruments) turned out to belong to Sovereen. Two of the witnesses testified that Sovereen could be violent when drinking.

The constable who arrested Sovereen testified to arriving at the scene about a half-hour after daybreak. He examined the bodies and the knife. He asked Sovereen if he could search him and Sovereen voluntarily gave him a knife that had blood on it. Sovereen said the blood came from his own fingers. He also found a club with several different colours of hair on it, but no blood.

Dr. Crouse, a surgeon, testified to going to the house and examining the bodies. The wife had received a blow to the head and a blow to the breastbone with a sharp pointed instrument, such as the knife that was found. He also examined Sovereen and said that his wounds looked self-inflicted and superficial.

The defence called no witnesses.[41]

Adjudication Records

Note: This inventory only contains records that begin before 1841. Many other records will be available for the post-1841 period.

Summary Conviction Records

There are very few records of summary convictions prior to 1833, when the law began requiring Justices of the Peace to prepare reports of their convictions and file them with the Clerk of the Peace before each Quarter Sessions sitting. Also, few records of police boards and Police Courts have survived. The listings below are those I have managed to discover. Others may be "buried" within the Quarter Sessions filings or Municipal council records.

Also check local newspapers for reports, especially after 1833.

Inventory

- AO RG 8-23 Provincial Secretary Records, Pre-Confederation Correspondence. These include many files of evidence when the way magistrates behaved in cases was in question, often the only evidence of summary convictions.
- AO RG 22-112 Western District (Windsor) Court of General Quarter Sessions of Peace, convictions 1835–1864 in Hiram Walker Collection, MS 205.
- PCMA Peterborough County Court fonds, 1830–1909: includes convictions.
- TUA 90-005 Victoria County fonds, 1834–1969: General Quarter Sessions of the Peace, includes convictions.
- TUA United Counties of Northumberland and Durham. Court records fonds, 1803–1955: General Quarter Sessions of the Peace, includes conviction returns, magistrate's returns.
- MUML Marjorie Freeman Campbell Collection, Typescript of Hamilton Police Village Minutes, 1833–1850.
- QUA Prescott Police Board Minute books, 1834–1850. Microfilmed copy of original in vault of the Prescott municipal offices.
- TUA 90-005 Victoria County fonds, 1834–1969: General Quarter Sessions of the Peace, includes Police Court records.

Court Minute Books

Minute books are organized chronologically by session. At the start of each session, the location of the court and the date is recorded, along with the name(s) of the presiding judge(s) or magistrates, and the grand jurors. Next, there is a list of indictments considered by the grand jury, indicating "no bill" or "true bill" for each. After all the indictments are registered, the individual cases are recorded. Early minute books contain only the barest of information about each case:

- the date and place of the trial;
- the charge;
- the names of the accused;
- the names of members of the jury;
- the plea; and
- the verdict (often left to the end of the session and listed with other sentences).

Sometimes, you'll also get a list of witness, usually divided into "pro" (on the side of the prosecutor) and "def" (on the side of the defendant). Later minutes can include details of the alleged offence, bail conditions, the name of the defence counsel, and lists of exhibits. Each volume usually has an index in alphabetical order by the defendant's last name.

In some cases, you may find "draft" minutes surviving. These are usually messier and more difficult to read, but they can also be more informative than the final official minutes. The Toronto Mayor's Court records are a case in point. The polished official minutes are beautiful to read, but spare in the information they provide. The draft minutes are ugly, but full of detailed descriptions of the testimony of the witnesses.

Minute books for police boards seem to be far more detailed than those for the Quarter Sessions, Mayor's Courts, and Assizes. They may contain verbatim transcripts of all the testimony. Surviving records are sparse — I only know of Prescott, Toronto, and Hamilton surviving (however, others might be "hiding" within "council" records). Minutes are also called "proceedings."

Inventory

Assize (High Court)

*   AO RG 22-134 Court of King's/Queen's Bench Criminal Assize minute books, 1792–1848, MS 530 Reels 1-4 (entire province).
*   AO RG 22-135 Court of King's/Queen's Bench Criminal Assize rough minute books, 1792–1849.
*   TPL Assizes of Upper Canada. Minutes by the Clerk of the Assize, R. Hervey Jr.

    *   London District, 23–25 May 1837
    *   Bathurst District, 19–23 September 1837
    *   Prince Edward District, 27–30 September 1837
    *   Midland District, 3–14 October 1837

*   TUA United Counties of Northumberland and Durham. Court records fonds, 1803–1955: includes Court of Queen's Bench records.
*   Corupe, Linda. *Upper Canadian Justice (early Assize Court Records of Ontario), Volume 1 (1792–1809)*. Bolton, ON: Linda Corupe, 2004. Complete transcriptions of the cases of the Court of Oyer and Terminer and General Gaol Delivery for the entire Province of Upper Canada, including verdicts, jury lists, and sureties; they also contains extensive appendices and end notes.
*   Corupe, Linda. *Upper Canadian Justice (early Assize Court Records of Ontario), Volume 2 (1810–1818)*. Bolton, ON: Linda Corupe, 2008. This volume contains several

historically important and renowned trials from the period, such as the Ancaster "Bloody Assize" of 1814 (the trials of those accused of treason during the War of 1812–1814).

Quarter Sessions
- AO RG 22-09 Hastings County (Belleville) Court of General Quarter Sessions of Peace, minutes, 1837–1866.
- AO RG 22-12 Leeds and Grenville United Counties (Brockville), Court of General Quarter Sessions of Peace minutes, 1800–1956, MS 699 Reels 1–4.
- UWO B155 London District Quarter Sessions Records, miscellaneous papers, 1831–1846.
- AO RG 22-29 Newcastle District (Cobourg) Court of General Quarter Sessions of Peace minutes, 1802–1893, MS 698, Reels 1–2.
- AO RG 22-54 Midland District (Kingston) Court of General Quarter Sessions of Peace minutes, 1800–1849, MS 694.
- AO RG 22-65 Ottawa District (L'Orignal) Court of General Quarter Sessions of Peace minutes, 1816–1869, MS 697 Reels 1–2.
- AO RG 22-75 Lanark County (Perth) Court of General Quarter Sessions of Peace minutes, 1823–1896, MS 696.
- AO RG 22-83 Prince Edward County (Picton), Court of General Quarter Sessions of Peace minutes, 1834–1908, MS 695.
- AO RG 22-94 York County/Home District (York/Toronto) Court of General Quarter Sessions of Peace minutes, 1800–1957, MS 251.
- AO RG 22-95 Home District (Toronto) Court of General Quarter Sessions of Peace rough minutes, 1836–1917.

- AO RG 22-103 Essex County (Windsor) Court of General Quarter Sessions of Peace minutes, 1821–1886, MS 166.
- AO RG 22-107 Western District (Windsor) Court of General Quarter Sessions of Peace, rough minutes, 1835–1859 in Hiram Walker Collection, MS 205.
- AO RG 22-108 Western District (Windsor) Court of General Quarter Sessions of Peace, minutes of the chairman, 1836–1845 in Hiram Walker Collection, MS 205.
- AO RG 22-372 Lincoln County/Niagara District (Niagara) Court of General Quarter Sessions of Peace minutes, 1828–1919.
- LAC MG9 D8-8 Records Relating to the Eastern District: Record book of the Court of General Quarter Session of Peace, 1826–1849.
- LAC MG9 D8-20 London District papers, Court of General Quarter Sessions of the Peace, London District 1800–1809, proceedings (photocopy).
- LAC MG9 D8-21 Court of General Quarter Sessions of the Peace, Luneburg District 1789–1827, proceedings (photocopy).
- LAC MG9 D8-33 Proceedings of the Court of General Quarter Sessions of the Peace, Western District 1799–1802, 37 pages.
- LSUC PF16-1 Luneburg District [Eastern] - Court of General Quarter Sessions of the Peace minute book, 1789–1802.
- LSUC PF16-2 Mecklenburg District [Midland] - Court of General Quarter Sessions of the Peace minute books, 1789–1827.
- QUA Upper Canada. Court of Quarter Sessions fonds, 1790–1816. Mecklenburg Quarter Session, 1790–1816

and Lunenburg Quarter Session, 1789–1802. Microfilm copy of originals in Law Society of Upper Canada.

- TPL General Quarter Sessions of the Peace for the Home District, Minutes, 13 March 1800–17 October 1801, in handwriting of Thomas Ridout, slightly more abbreviated than the copy at the Archives of Ontario.
- TPL General Quarter Sessions of the Peace for the Home District, Minutes, 10 April 1801–7 February 1867, 16 volumes of typewritten transcripts, copy made in 1910.
- TPL General Quarter Sessions of the Peace for the London District, Minutes, 1800–1809, printed.
- UWO B636 Minutes of the Court of Quarter Sessions, London District, 1813–1820, Volume 62, including sub-ject index (minutes transcribed by Frank Clark).
- UWO M779-M780 London District Court of Quarter Sessions, minutes, 1814–1853, microfilm.
- UWO M1247 London District Court of Quarter Sessions, minute book, 1800–1809, microfilm.
- TUA 90-005 Victoria County fonds, 1834–1969: General Quarter Sessions of the Peace, County Criminal Courts, sheriff's books, Police Court, Inquests, Convictions, Juries, Accounts (majority are post-1860).
- TUA United Counties of Northumberland and Durham. Court records fonds, 1803–1955: General Quarter Sessions of the Peace, Court of Queen's Bench, Indictment and Conviction Returns, Oaths of Coroners and Jail Surgeons, Commissions of Coroners and Magistrates, Coroner's Inquests, Juror rolls and jury lists, Magistrate's returns.
- Corupe, Linda. *Minutes of the Court of Quarter Sessions of the Peace, Mecklenburg/ Midland District. Volume 1: 1789–1816.* Bolton, ON: Linda Corupe, [c2001]. A transcription of the court cases, jury lists, tavern and

ferry applications, road work approvals, land transactions, municipal business, etc.

- Corupe, Linda. *Minutes of the Court of Quarter Sessions of the Peace, Midland District, Volume 2: 1832–1840*. Bolton, ON: Linda Corupe, 2001.
  - Corupe, Linda. *Minutes of the Court of Quarter Sessions of the Peace, Midland District, Volume 3: 1841–1849*. Bolton, ON: Linda Corupe, 2002.
  - "Minutes of the Court of General Quarter Sessions of the Peace for the London District, 1 April, 1800 to 12 September, 1809 and 4 December, 1813 to 26 December, 1818," *Twenty-Second Report of the Department of Public Records and Archives of Ontario* edited by Alexander Fraser, 1933.
- "Minutes of the Court of General Quarter Sessions of the Peace for the Home District, 13th March, 1800 to 28th December, 1811," *Twenty-First Report of the Department of Public Records and Archives of Ontario*, edited by Alexander Fraser, 1932.

Mayor's Court

- TCA fonds 95 (formerly RG7 Series E) Toronto Mayor's Court fonds:
- Proceedings, 2 June 1834–4 Sept 1838 (beautifully clear).
- Draft proceedings 1837–1841 and 1843–1846 (rough, but including very detailed descriptions of the evidence, not found in the final proceedings).

Case Files or Filings

A far more detailed set of court records are the case filings or files.

These can contain a wide range of documents prepared in the course of the investigation and trial. They can include: recognizances, summonses, warrants, informations, examinations, indictments, police reports, exhibits such as maps or photographs, coroner's records, and lists of evidence. They can be called "files," "case files," and "filings."

Inventory

Assizes (High Court)

- AO RG 4-1, Boxes 6-7 Crown Prosecutions Case files, 1799–1843.
- AO RG 22-138 Court of King's Bench Criminal Assize Filings, 1792–1799, 1815–1819. These are all indexed in the ADD by defendant's name, a total of twenty-seven cases, plus a file of recognizances for the Eastern District, 1798/1799.
- TPL L16 William Dummer Powell papers, B85: bound book "Circuit Papers" 1788–1820. Includes miscellaneous papers relating to a wide range of cases, including affidavits, a coroner's inquest, and indictment, an information, a jury summons, and several petitions.

Quarter Sessions

- AO RG 22-14 Johnstown District (Brockville), Court of General Quarter Sessions of Peace, Case Files, 1802–1846.
- AO RG 22-32 Newcastle District (Cobourg) Court of General Quarter Sessions of the Peace filings, 1803–1848. Consists of filings, such as recognizances, summonses, warrants, informations, and examinations, of the Court of General Sessions of the Peace for the Newcastle District. Also included in this series are jurors' excuses

for non-attendance at Sessions. From 1836 to 1847 filings also contain criminal Assize summonses. These were probably submitted to the court by the constables for payment of their fees. Documents are organized chronologically by year. There are no records for 1845 or 1847.

- AO RG 22-96 York County (York/Toronto) Court of General Sessions of the Peace filings — only a smattering of documents for the years 1796–1799, 1828, 1832, 1838. Include informations, examinations, warrants, recognizances, depositions.

- AO RG 22-109 Western District (Windsor) Court of General Quarter Sessions of Peace, case files, 1821–1859 in Hiram Walker Collection, MS 205.

- AO RG 22-110 Western District (Windsor) Court of General Quarter Sessions of Peace, filings, 1822–1859 in Hiram Walker Collection, MS 205.

- AO RG 22-120 Western District (Windsor) Court of General Quarter Sessions of Peace, miscellaneous, 1808–1853 in Hiram Walker Collection, MS 205.

- AO RG 22-372 Lincoln County/Niagara District (St. Catharines) Court of General Quarter Sessions of Peace filings, 1828–1919.

- TUA 90-005 Victoria County fonds, 1834–1969: General Quarter Sessions of the Peace records.

- TUA United Counties of Northumberland and Durham. Court records fonds, 1803–1955: General Quarter Sessions of the Peace, Court of Queen's Bench, Indictment and Conviction Returns, Oaths of Coroners and Jail Surgeons, Commissions of Coroners and Magistrates, Coroner's Inquests, Juror rolls and jury lists, Magistrate's returns.

Assize Judge's Benchbooks

The bench books of the presiding judge should always be investigated, as they provide a great deal more information than you will find in the official court records. These notebooks generally contain almost verbatim testimony of all the witnesses. The main difficulty you will have with these records is that they weren't meant to be public, so they're often written in hasty, messy handwriting.

Inventory

- AO RG 22-390-1 Bench books of James B. Macaulay, 1827–1857.
- AO RG 22-390-2 Bench books of Sir John B. Robinson, 1829–1863.
- AO RG 22-390-3 Bench books of Christopher Hagerman, 1828–1829.
- AO RG 22-390-4 Bench books of Jonas Jones, 1837–1848.

Government Correspondence

Inventory

- LAC RG 5 A1 Civil secretary, Correspondence (incoming) also known as the Upper Canada Sundries.
- LAC RG 5 A2 Civil secretary, Correspondence (outgoing), drafts of replies.
- LAC RG 7 G16 Civil secretary, Correspondence (outgoing), replies sent.
- LAC R188-36-2-E (formerly RG13-F-1) Dept of

Justice fonds, Office of the Attorney General of Canada West, 1800–1866. Series consists of correspondence, authorizations, and legal documents relating to matters under the supervision of the Attorney General of Canada West and his predecessor the Attorney General of Upper Canada. These papers include a large number of fiats, memorials, and petitions; papers of the Legislative Assembly; and material regarding civil and criminal cases.

- AO RG 22-768: Correspondence of the Clerks of the Crown, 1825–1869, includes incoming letters and letterbooks.
- AO RG 22-119 Essex County (Windsor) Court of General Quarter Sessions of Peace, correspondence, 1792–1881 in Hiram Walker Collection, MS 205.
- TCA fonds 200 Series 362 (formerly RG7 Series B) Mayor's Office Letterbook, November 1834 to July 1844. Contains 406 letters, many of which refer to Mayor's Court matters.

Private Papers

You may find evidence of arbitration without going to court, in private papers of magistrates, Clerks of the Peace, and sheriffs.

If the defendant was represented by council, there may also be records kept by his lawyer or the law firm of which he was a member. The Archives of Ontario has a few private papers of lawyers and law firms. Others may be held in municipal, county, and regional archives, as well as private hands.

Assize Judges

- TPL L16 William Dummer Powell papers:

  - B85: bound book "Circuit Papers" 1788–1820. Includes miscellaneous papers relating to a wide range of cases, including affidavits, a coroner's inquest, and indictment, an information, a jury summons, and several petitions.
  - B87: Papers regarding prisoners and trials throughout Upper Canada, 1794–1825. Mostly calendars of prisoners, also a few jury lists.
  - Unbound legal papers and notebooks: includes one bound bail book, dated 1803 (seems to be the start date, goes up to at least 1808), and rough minutes for Assize sessions from 1818 to 1825 (these seem to be his version of a judges' bench book, some begin with his charge to the grand jury). Some are not clearly identified by district and date, but close examination of the contents should help identify this. The ones I could quickly identify are as follows:

    - London District, August 1818
    - Newcastle District, Michaelmas Term 1819
    - Hilary Term 1820
    - Easter Term 1820
    - Trinity Term 1820
    - Midland District, August–September 1820
    - Home District, 16 October 1820
    - Midland District, August 1825

- Johnston District, August 1825
- Eastern District, August 1825

- LSUC PF 8 William Osgoode collection, 1772–1824. Collection consists of correspondence received and sent by William Osgoode, first Chief Justice of Upper Canada. The collection consists of two bound volumes entitled: "Osgoode Correspondence 1772–1823," and loose correspondence. The majority of the letters relate to Osgoode's personal life, and only a few date from his time in Canada. The letters have been published in: *Friends of the Chief Justice: The Osgoode Correspondence in the Archives of the Law Society of Upper Canada*, edited by Douglas Hay and Ruth Paley, The Law Society of Upper Canada, Toronto, 1990.

- LAC R4419-0-0-E (formerly MG24 I57) 1833–1834, Robert Lyon collection. Collection consists of recollections of a Mr. Cromwell containing an account of the duel between John Wilson and Robert Lyon, photocopy, 1833, three pages; extracts from a notebook attributed to Chief Justice John Beverley Robinson [This is incorrect; it was probably Judge Macaulay.] relating to the trial of John Wilson and Simon Robertson for the killing of Robert Lyon in a duel, a case over which the Hon. Mr. Justice Macaulay presided, transcript, 1834, twelve pages.

Justices of the Peace

- LAC R3800-0-3-E (formerly MG24 D108) Robert Nelles fonds 1782–1848. Series consists of chronologically arranged papers of Robert Nelles and his family. The reports and affidavits largely pertain to his career and activities as a Member of Legislative Assembly and a Justice of the Peace respectively.

- NHS Records of Justice of the Peace, Francis Leigh Walsh (1824–1880).
- TPL S113 Alexander Wood papers, 1798–1837. Correspondence and court filings while Justice of the Peace in York, 180 pieces.
- TUA 71-006 John Huston fonds, 1818–1849. Includes his papers as Justice of the Peace.

Clerks of the Peace

- LAC MG 9 D8-14 Johnstown District collection: the papers of Edward Jessup, Clerk of the Peace 1800–1801, 102 pages. Series consists of papers preserved by Edward Jessup while Clerk of the Peace. Included are memorials of Edward Jessup and Sheriff Thomas Fraser for compensation for services, 1800–1801, eight pages; a letter from Jessup to the magistrates concerning the completion of the assessment rolls, 28 January 1801, two pages; and miscellaneous papers relating to prosecutions before the Court of General Quarter Sessions of the Peace for the Johnstown District. A list of individuals involved precedes the volumes, 92 pages.
- NHS Thomas Welch Papers, Clerk of the Court, London District. Court papers, 1796–1816.
- PCMA Peterborough County Court fonds, 1830–1909: Clerk of the Peace Records; Criminal Court cases; indictments; convictions.

Sheriffs

- LAC R4029-0-2-E (formerly MG 24 I8) MacDonell Family Fonds, Allan MacDonell papers, 1837–1868. Series consists of papers and records collected as sheriff of Gore, 1837–1843, relating primarily to the Rebellion of 1837.

- LAC R4024-0-6-E (formerly MG 24 I26 volumes 44–48) Alexander Hamilton and family fonds, records of the sheriff and various courts of the Niagara District, 1818–1837.
- LAC R6180-0-5-E (formerly MG 24 I27) John McEwan fonds, 1811–1868. Fonds consists of correspondence and papers of Captain John McEwan, including some legal documents acquired while he was sheriff of Essex County.
- LAC R3944-0-4-E (formerly MG 24 I73) J. W. Dunbar Moodie fonds. Official correspondance received by Moodie while he was sheriff of the Victoria District 1839–1863.
- TUA 90-005 Victoria County fonds, 1834–1969: General Quarter Sessions of the Peace, includes sheriff's books.

Rebellion Records and Treason Trials

Records of investigations for treason and rebellion are often found separated from regular criminal records. Known collections are as follows.

Inventory

Treason Trials
- AO RG 22-134 Central Criminal Assize minute books, Volume 4, pages 153–167 for minutes of Ancaster Treason Trials.
- AO RG 22-143 Court of King's Bench records of high treason trial of 1814, 1814–1824. Series consists of the few remaining records of the High Treason Trials held

at Ancaster during May and June 1814. Included are the following documents: dockets regarding the outlawry of Matthias Brown and Benajah Mallory; two depositions against Eliazir Daggett, Oliver Gran, and Eliakim Crosby; and the indictment against Luther McNeal and an exemplification of judgment against McNeal. Also included with this series are the commissions and inquisitions regarding lands forfeited by those convicted of high treason. The commissions were issued in December 1817, and the inquisitions were held in January 1818. There is also a commission and inquisition for Samuel Thompson dated 1824.

- AO RG 22-144 Alien Act Commissions, inquisitions and related records, 1815–1830.
- AO RG 22-145: Court of King's Bench record of high treason trials of 1838: Series consists of the only court records available for the High Treason Trials of 1838, as the court proceedings were not recorded in the criminal Assize minute books for that year. The files consist of a court order for the charge of high treason issued against Ebenezer Wilcox on 6 August 1838, and indictments for treason issued against John Stewart the Younger in March 1838 and William Ketchum in August 1838.

Rebellion Records

- LAC RG 5 B36, B37 Civil Secretary, records relating to rebellions. Upper Canada. The special files of records relating to the Rebellions of 1837–1838 consist of minutes of proceedings for the trials conducted by the magistrates, 1837–1838, and the proceedings of the militia courts martial, 1838–1839, for the London District.

- LAC RG 5 B38 Civil Secretary, records relating to rebellions. Upper Canada. Contemporary copies of the 1839 proceedings in the Court of Queen's Bench in England resulting in the release of ten out of twenty-three men from the Niagara District intended for transportation to Australia.
- LAC RG 5 B39 Civil Secretary, records relating to rebellions. Upper Canada. Records of the inquiry into the conduct of Colonel John Prince at the Battle of Windsor, 1839.
- LAC RG 5 B40, B41 Civil Secretary, records relating to rebellions. Upper Canada. Proceedings of the courts martial at Fort Henry, Kingston, 1838–1839.
- LAC RG 5 B43 Civil Secretary, records relating to Rebellions. Upper Canada. Documents relating to the prosecution of Alexander McLeod for the destruction of the *Caroline*, 1841.
- LAC R4029-0-2-E (formerly MG 24 I8) MacDonell Family Fonds, Allan MacDonell papers, 1837–1868. Series consists of papers and records collected as sheriff of Gore, 1837–1843 relating primarily to the Rebellion of 1837.

CHAPTER FOUR

Sentencing and Punishment

From the time of its founding in 1791, Upper Canada was a British colony, ruled by British law. While it was possible to enact new laws by modifying those inherited from Britain, very few actual changes were made until 1833.[1] What this meant was that until the 1830s Upper Canada punished crimes by means of a "traditional mix" of penalties including shaming (whipping and stocks), fines, banishment and transportation, imprisonment, and execution.

Between 1792 and 1830 there were 737 convictions at the Assizes: 162 received gaol (jail) only, 114 received capital punishment, 109 received corporal punishment and gaol, 132 received fine and gaol, sixty-three received just a fine, eighty-one were banished, forty-eight were to stand in the stocks.[2]

Based on the records of the Home and London Districts, punishments at the Quarter Sessions seem to have been much lighter than those meted out at the Assizes. At the Quarter Sessions the majority of offenders received only fines. There was frequent use of recognizances of the peace for assault. Gaol was used in less than 10 percent of cases and even then it was only for very brief periods. There was no whipping, pillory, or banishments.[3] Starting in the 1830s, sentencing policy began to shift to a more modern approach relying heavily upon incarceration.[4]

Peace Bonds

A frequent alternative to punitive sentences was the "peace bond" or "recognizance of the peace." The magistrate imposed a period of up to twelve months wherein the offender had to "keep the peace" with whomever he/she was accused of assaulting or harassing. Two other people had to post expensive bonds as sureties. They would lose their money if the person "broke the peace" (i.e., got in another fight), so the bond gave them good incentive to exert social pressure on the offender to behave.

Peace bonds weren't actually sentences, as they were usually imposed without conviction, but they were an important tool in the magistrates' arsenal.

Recognizances of the Peace were frequently used in cases of domestic assault. For example, in December 1838, William Cochrane of Wainfleet Township attacked his wife of thirteen years, Elizabeth, throwing her to the floor and choking her. When her son intervened, saving her life (so she believed), she fled the home and went to stay with her neighbours. The town wardens filed a statement with the Niagara Clerk of the Peace stating that in their belief that Cochrane was "a man of unsound mind and a Dangerous Character to go at Large," thus justifying his incarceration in the local gaol. Elizabeth herself did not file a complaint until several months later, after the magistrate had issued a warrant to commit Cochrane to gaol for refusing to keep the peace with his wife. In her statement she described the December incident, emphasizing that she was not complaining "out of any hatred, malice or ill-will ... but purely for the preservation of her person and children from further danger."[5] Cochrane finally agreed to sign a recognizance for £20 to keep the peace towards Elizabeth. It appears that the magistrates did not want to prosecute him for domestic assault (such prosecutions were rare and usually unsuccessful), but the wardens did their best to protect Elizabeth by claiming that her husband was insane and should be kept in jail. Their tactic failed, but perhaps the prospect of losing the £20 (and incurring the wrath of his two sureties, who each had to put up £10), offered Elizabeth some protection.[6]

Fines

Fines were frequently used by the Court of Quarter Sessions, but were of limited value as people often couldn't pay. Sometimes fines were abused — convicts were ordered gaoled until they paid the fine, but since they couldn't pay, they ended up spending months, even years in gaol.[7]

Magistrates had wide latitude in the amount of fine to impose and it showed in the records. For example, of twenty convictions for assault and battery in the London District Quarter Sessions from 1800 to 1809, the fines ranged from 1s. to £7 (the average was 5s., or about $129 today).[8]

In addition to the actual fine, those convicted were usually required to pay the court's costs. These are difficult to estimate, as they depend on how many witnesses had to be summoned, examined, and paid for their appearance, how far the witnesses had to travel, how far the constables had to travel to serve the summons, whether an arrest warrant or recognizances were issued, and so on. In some cases, the court costs would greatly exceed the actual fine.

The proceeds from fines were generally supposed to be put towards local administrative expenses, such as the improvement of the roads, but there was some flexibility in this. For example, in 1839 two Oxford County magistrates, John Weir and George Whitehead, convicted William Cruden of assaulting his nineteen-year-old servant girl, Julia Higgins. They imposed the heaviest fine they were allowed without taking the case to the Quarter Sessions: £5.

If the assault had been of the typical kind, such as a bar brawl, that would have been excessive. But the victim had been beaten so badly that she was unable to walk. When the magistrates saw her, she was "naked, filthy and full of bruises so much so one would hardly suppose her a human being." Several witnesses had testified to the brutality she had suffered.

The magistrates were later accused of pocketing the fine money, because it didn't appear in the clerk's books. They explained that it had been used to pay the doctor who treated the victim and the people who looked after her while she was recovering.[9]

Branding and Whipping

Up until 1802, convicts could be branded (burned on the hand) for a variety of offences, including petty theft. In 1802 the practice was abolished, except in cases of manslaughter.[10]

Public flogging or whipping was a frequently used punishment up until the 1830s, with the most common number of lashes being thirty-nine, probably following biblical precedent.[11] At the Assizes, whipping was the preferred punishment for petty thieves, usually combined with brief gaol sentences. Whipping sentences dropped sharply in the 1830s. However, for many years it continued to be used within gaols.[12]

A Whipping Frame, *James Edmund Jones,* Pioneer Crimes and Punishment, *Toronto: George N. Morang, 1924, 23.*

The Lieutenant-Governor received a great many petitions for mercy from people sentenced to public flogging, which were frequently granted. It appears that of all the punishments, flogging was considered the most shameful.[13]

Stocks and Pillory

Stocks were wooden contraptions with holes for arms (if standing) or legs (if sitting). The pillory was like the stocks but included a hole for the neck. As with the other "shaming" punishments, the stocks were commonly used in the early years of Upper Canada, but gradually fell out of favour in the mid-1830s and were abolished (along with the pillory) in 1841.[14]

Before it fell out of use, the pillory was often used by the Quarter Sessions as punishment for minor thefts, commonly for periods of an hour.[15] For example, at the Quarter Sessions Peter Thomas Surplus was found guilty of larceny for "stealing a pair of shoes" in January 1830. His sentence was to "stand in the pillory for one hour tomorrow, 12 o'clock, in the public square." That same session, James Aldridge was sentenced to be put in the stocks for two hours, and to pay £2 1s. 5d. for trespass and assault.[16]

One of the reasons for discontinuing the pillory's use was that it encouraged public discord. If sentence was considered too light, people would assault the prisoner while he was immobilized; if they thought it was too harsh, they might release him — and if there was disagreement, riots could ensue.[17]

The *History of the County of Middlesex* provides the following example:

> On one occasion there were two men in the stocks for stealing turkeys, and the curious people when gathered there or in passing the culprits, themselves made a noise such as a hen turkey calling her brood around would make.
>
> John McLoughlin, the wrecker, a powerful Irishman, who was an early shoemaker here, came down to the stocks on ??? day. Seeing the

turkey stealers in the ugly frame, he asked Peter Schram: "Arrah, Peach, what are you doin' with these poor devils here." Schram responded, telling the cause, but McLoughlin kicked out the wedges, determined to set the prisoners free. Schram cautioned him saying: "If you do not behave yourself, John, you'll get there yourself," while Sheriff Rapelje, who was near, approved Constable Schram's warning. McLoughlin saw the point and walking away said, "Sheriff, punish the men decently, but don't make a show for the whole town."[18]

Banishment

Serious crimes that might otherwise entail capital punishment were often punished by banishment instead. There was some flexibility in the sentence in that it could be for a limited time period (as little as a few months, in some cases) or for life. It could also apply only to a limited jurisdiction (such as the town, county or district) or to the entire country.[19]

For example, Charlotte Lee, the widow of an army sergeant, was convicted of keeping a disorderly house in Toronto in June 1834. The offence was a misdemeanor and she was fined £1 and banished from her "house and neighbourhood" (no time period was stated, so presumably it was meant to be permanent). She was given one week to pack up and leave. She also had to sign a recognizance for £20 to keep the peace for six months, and get two sureties to also sign recognizances for £10 each.[20] The sentence was rather lenient, but the newspaper account of the trial explained that the jury had recommended mercy due to the fact that she had lost her husband to cholera, was destitute and needed to provide for her children, and was far from home (England) without any support.[21]

Banishment was a practical sentence, often used during the early period in Upper Canada, when the public was becoming less and less approving of capital punishment, and gaols were extremely expensive to build and maintain. However, if enforced, it could ruin a person's life and livelihood. A farmer would lose the benefit of all his hard work in clearing his land and building up his farm; a merchant would lose all of his customers; families were uprooted and separated from everyone they knew. William Lyon Mackenzie suffered banishment after his failed rebellion in 1837. When he was finally permitted to return to Upper Canada from New York he was a broken man, no longer the fiery critic of the government he had been.[22]

However, banishment was difficult to enforce, and many people thus sentenced never even left the province, or returned well before their time was up, without repercussions. It was pretty much up to the local community to draw attention to these facts — if the community did not do so, the convict often went virtually free.

Execution

The ultimate form of punishment was execution. In Upper Canada that meant death by public hanging. Responsibility for carrying out the sentence was vested in the sheriff, who hired a hangman to do the job. The fact that there were only one or two hangings in the entire colony each year generally meant that hangmen were inexperienced, and the job was often botched.[23]

The execution of Michael Vincent in 1828 was a case in point.

The Public Hangings of Samuel Lount and Peter Mathews, Toronto, *1838, James Edmund Jones,* Pioneer Crimes and Punishment, *Toronto: George N. Morang, 1924.*

On the morning of 8 September … [he was] brought up from his cell in the log basement. For his short walk, his legs were freed of chains.

After the cavalry had formed its line, the magistrates, the grand jury, and leading gentlemen approached the courthouse in a column by pairs. Once they were all assembled, Michael Vincent stopped out of a window and onto the gallows platform. He was asked if he had any final words. The boy, his parents, and all others heard him proclaim: "I died innocent before God and man." The executioner — a black man — loosened Vincent's shirt at the neck and placed a thick rope noose over his head. Vincent went stiff with terror. No hood covered his face; some spectators could see the expression of horror.... The drop failed to break Vincent's neck. The knot had slipped around to the front below the chin; it pulled the man's head backward. He was strangling. Writhing in pain, he swung his feet in desperation, attempting to reach the log ledge where the upper and lower floors of the court-house met. To finish his botched job, the executioner grabbed the legs and jerked them down sharply. Vincent continued to struggle. Hugging the swinging figure, the executioner added his own weight to that of the dying Vincent. Curses from the crowd denouncing the executioner declared that this execution had forfeited the dramatic effect desired by all authorities who staged such proceedings. The condemned man had not performed the role expected of him; he had protested his innocence and this had unsettled some people. Then came the miserable job of the hanging, which transformed Vincent from a convicted wife-murderer into the victim of a dreadfully violent death.[24]

Nonetheless, people flocked to watch these gruesome affairs. "In 1830, over 3,000 people converged on the tiny village of London, then barely 300 souls, to witness the district's first public execution."[25]

Capital punishment was reserved for the most serious offences, but in 1820 that still included a lengthy list of 120 crimes. In 1833 the list was reduced to twelve: high treason, murder, petit treason, rescuing persons convicted of or committed for murder, carnal knowledge of a girl under ten years of age, sodomy, robbery, robbing the mail, burglary, arson, and accessory before the fact of any of the aforelisted offences.[26] In 1841, the list was reduced to six: murder, treason, rape, sodomy, carnal knowledge of a girl under ten years of age, and poisoning with intent to murder.[27]

Between 1792 and 1869, 392 people were sentenced to death by hanging (fifty-eight for murder, most of the rest for treason), but only ninety-two were actually executed. The rest had their sentences commuted to banishment or to a life sentence in the penitentiary.[28]

For example, of the fourteen people sentenced to death in the Gore District between 1822 and 1841, only one was executed. He had been convicted of murdering his wife. Three were banished. Their crimes were "shooting," rape, and murder. One died in gaol. Two were sent to Kingston Penitentiary (both for "shooting"). Seven were shown "mercy" (their crimes included "shooting," riot, horse theft, and theft of a steer).[29]

Despite the opportunity for mercy, as time wore on many juries refused to convict for capital offences.[30] This was one of the reasons driving sentencing reform in the 1830s, and the building of Kingston Penitentiary (i.e., to provide an alternative to capital punishment for dangerous criminals).

Imprisonment

The final sentencing option was imprisonment. The first session of the Upper Canada legislature passed a statute requiring each district to erect a gaol (jail) and courthouse at its own expense. But there were no rules guiding their structure or governance. Construction and administration of these was, by far, the single greatest strain on the district government budgets. While they

THE FIRST GAOL IN YORK, 1800-1824
From the J. Ross Robertson Collection

The First Gaol In York, 1800–1824, *James Edmund Jones,* Pioneer Crimes and Punishment, *Toronto: George N. Morang, 1924, 48.*

did their best to build impressive-looking, solidly constructed edifices, most of the early gaols were very small, usually occupying the same building as the courthouse.

At first, there were only four districts: Eastern, Midland, Home, and Western. The gaols/courthouses were naturally built in their administrative centres: Cornwall, Kingston, Newark [Niagara-on-the-Lake], and Sandwich [Windsor].[31]

The Midland District was the first to have a purpose-built edifice. Completed in 1793, its two-storey stone courthouse and gaol was used until 1833.[32] By 1799 all four of the original districts had new structures, and the new districts soon followed suit.

We know the most about the first York/Toronto gaol (the centre of the Home District was moved from Newark to York in 1801): it was opened in early 1799; it was thirty-four feet by twenty feet, built of squared logs ten inches thick; it was divided into three rooms and had two floors. A few years later a stockade was built around it. Larger than most, the gaol was

The Old Court House and Gaol in Dundas, Ontario. A Prehistoric Court House, *J. R. Seavey,* Wentworth Landmarks, *Hamilton: Spectator Printing Company, 1897.*

paid for by the Executive Council of Upper Canada because it served the capital.[33]

By 1841 there were twenty districts in Upper Canada, each with its own courthouse and gaol.[34] The later structures were a little larger, generally comprising several large cells for criminal prisoners, several for debtors, and quarters for the gaoler and his family.[35]

As noted, until gaol reform in 1838, each district had considerable autonomy. There were no province-wide standards. The Justices of the Peace in the Quarter Sessions determined the salaries of the gaoler and rules and regulations for operation of the gaols, such as the type and quantity of food, bedding, clothing, and wood provided.[36]

Who Was Imprisoned?

Tight budgets, and the fact that the gaols were multi-purpose, meant that the gaols were almost always crowded. At first, they weren't even intended as punishment, just as temporary places to hold people while they awaited trial or other punishments. However, they also held debtors who couldn't pay up, people who were considered dangerous or unable to look after themselves (such as the insane and the deaf and dumb), vagrants, and overly intoxicated people.[37] Many argued that keeping all those different people together, not even separating men from women (or indeed, children), was unjust and unwise, but it would be until the mid-1830s before dedicated institutions began to be built for the poor, the insane, the sick, and the dangerously criminal.[38]

In fact, there was no separate asylum for the insane or for the deaf and dumb until the provincial lunatic asylum opened in 1846.[39] While they were housed in gaols, grand juries sometimes successfully argued for extra funds for food and clothing for the "maniacs" and "lunatics."[40]

One horrific case exemplifies the problem: Patrick Donnelly was an Irish immigrant charged with murdering his wife in September 1832. He was never convicted because Chief Justice Robinson and the petit jury for the trial judged him to be insane and thus incapable to standing trial. He was brought to the jail just prior to the September Assizes in 1832, and remained in jail until his death in 1840 — longer than any other prisoner in the history of the Niagara jail. While there were many doubts about his insanity, some believed it was just an act, no one knew what to do with him. Just about everyone was sure he wasn't safe to release, but it was expensive to keep him in the jail, so there were several petitions sent to the provincial authorities asking for him to be moved elsewhere. But there wasn't anywhere else to

Cobourg Jail, Debtor Register, 1834. Administrative records of the Cobourg Jail, Archives of Ontario, RG 20-66.

send him. After he died in the jail, the jail surgeon conducted an autopsy (as was necessary any time a person died in custody). The report concluded that he died of an epileptic seizure.[41]

The problem of dealing the debtors was much more complicated. At first, debtors could be gaoled indefinitely — until they paid their debt or fines[42] — and the gaolors were often instructed not to feed them. Their families had to bring them whatever they needed. But this just made the problem worse; as long as they were in gaol the debtors had no way of earning wages to pay off their debts. The law was amended in 1805 to allow an imprisoned debtor, as long as he swore that he wasn't worth more than £5, to apply to the court to require his creditor to pay the gaoler 5s. a week for his maintenance.[43] This also discouraged creditors from prosecuting debtors who really couldn't pay.

Further reforms came in 1834, when new legislation provided that debtors confined for amounts under £10 might after thirty days in gaol could swear that they were worth less than the sum for which they were arrested and be discharged. By the same act, if they weren't worth more than £5, those owing £10 to £20 could apply for release after three months, those owing £20 to £100 could apply for release after six months, and those owing over £100 could apply for release after one year.[44] *But they weren't relieved of the debt!* In 1827, 60 percent of all prisoners were being held for debt.[45] As of 1836, 40 percent of all prisoners were still debtors.[46]

Gaol Conditions

Nineteenth-century gaols were horrific places. Crowding was the least of the indignities prisoners faced. In the early years, prisoners received only bread and water. Prisoners in the Home District gaol received one pound of bread per day.[47] In later years, they also received potatoes and small amount of meat.[48] If they could afford it, prisoners could purchase additional food and articles such as bedding, clothing, and soap from the district magistrate.[49] Distribution of the food was up to the discretion of the gaolor. Sometimes they distributed it in batches every two or three days.[50]

Most gaols were built of stone and prisoners were kept in the basement or the ground floor, so the cells were very damp and cold. Often the only protection prisoners had was a thin bed of straw and a blanket.[51] Gaols were not cleaned very often and generally stunk badly and were infested with lice and mice. The most common method of cleaning was to fumigate the cells with strong vinegar.[52]

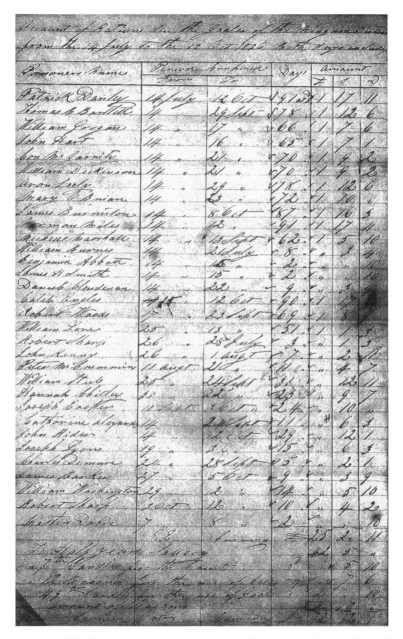

Account of Gaol rations, Administrative records of the Cobourg Jail, Archives of Ontario, RG 20-66.

Report of cases of sickness in the Niagara Goal during the year ending 31st Decr 1841 Accompanied by some remarks											
Greatest number of cases of sickness in the goal at one time 6				Total number of cases of sickness during the year 41				Deaths during the year 1			
Whites		Blacks Coloured p—		Whites		Blacks coloured p—		Whites		Blacks coloured p—	
M.	F	M.	F.	M.	F.	M.	F	M.	F	M.	F.
4	3	2	none	27	6	8	none	1	none	none	none

Gaol surgeon's report, Administrative records of the Cobourg Jail, Archives of Ontario, RG 20-66.

Between the crowding, the lack of fresh air, pure water, and nutritious foods, and the infrequency of cleaning, it is no wonder that there were frequent outbreaks of disease, plagues, and epidemics in the gaols. In fact, one of the names for typhus was "gaol fever."[53]

Even where the conditions were better and prisoners didn't get sick, a gaol sentence, even a brief one, could financially ruin a family, as there was no social assistance for families whose mother or father was imprisoned. Even women who were beaten within an inch of their lives, plead for the release of their husbands because they needed them for support.[54]

In one case a magistrate actually spent his own money to help the destitute wife of an imprisoned man. William Lyon Mackenzie (as mayor of Toronto in 1834, presiding over the Mayor's Court) sent the wife of a man he'd sentenced to gaol $2 for her support and so her husband couldn't use her destitution as an excuse for his release.[55]

Before he became mayor, Mackenzie had been an outspoken critic of gaol conditions. His 1830 report on the York Gaol described it thus:

> Your Committee found 25 persons in this prison, twelve criminals on the ground floor, one criminal sick up stairs, one vagrant, the three lunatics above mentioned, and nine debtors … The debtors are with one exception, all on the upper floor, apart from the other prisoners … These are allowed no support from their creditors, and some of them say they are entirely without the means of subsistence [*sic*]. James Colquhoun is in jail of a debt of three pounds; the creditor has forgiven the debt, but the lawyer has not thought proper to forgive him fees. Colquhoun subsists altogether on the humanity of the jailor and other debtors. One Murphy told your Committee that he had nothing to eat and that both Colquhoun and himself had been for days together, without tasting a morsel … One debtor is in jail, together with his wife, and a family of five children.[56]

Calendar of Prisoners, Newcastle Gaol, 1833. Archives of Ontario, RG 22-43, Envelope "1833–1835, Cobourg Gaol Records."

Calls for gaol reform culminated in the 1838 Act to Regulate the Future Erection of Gaols in This Province. The Act established a Board of Gaol Commissioners composed of Judges of the Court of King's Bench, the vice chancellor, all of the district sheriffs, and others appointed by the Lieutenant-Governor. They supervised the building of new gaols and formulated uniform rules and regulations for the administration of the gaols, including diet, clothing, bedding, medical care, religious instruction, restraint, and punishments.[57]

The new regulations divided prisoners into five classes and required heating, ventilation, and exercise for the prisoners. New registers were required to record fifteen pieces of information including age, occupation, education, place of birth, religion, offence, and conduct. Sample annual returns asked thirty-one questions in total.[58] Despite all these efforts, conditions in gaols continued to be horrific into the end of the century, and beyond.[59]

Kingston Penitentiary

For many reasons, hotly debated by historians, by the early 1830s Upper Canadian officials became convinced of the need for a provincial penitentiary. Kingston Penitentiary opened in June 1835.[60]

Some say Upper Canadians were becoming increasingly worried about the rise in crime and overcrowding in gaols — they wanted a larger, more secure place to send dangerous criminals.[61] According to the popular theories of the time, the main purpose of imprisonment was to punish offenders, secondarily to deter others and protect society. The aim of rehabilitation did not gain popularity until the 1840s.[62]

Others argue that there was no increase in crime nor fear thereof, what changed was that people started to want prisoners to be reformed and believed that a penitentiary would provide a central place to organize prisoners' labour, thus leading to their moral improvement through the cultivation of industrious habits.[63]

Another reason suggested was that juries had become reluctant to convict anyone if the sentence would be execution or lengthy gaol time, given the conditions in the gaols. Those who were convicted and sentenced frequently received pardons, for the same reasons. So they needed a new sentencing option.[64]

Whatever the reason behind the need for the penitentiary (and perhaps there were as many reasons as there were proponents), scholars agree that the building and planning for the administration of the penitentiary emulated the Auburn system, where convicts are kept strictly segregated from one another, not allowed to speak to one another when together, and kept busy with hard labour. Once the penitentiary was completed it was to hold 800 convicts, whose labour would completely pay for the operation of the prison. There were even suggestions that convicts could even be used to build the later phases.[65]

Terrance Lynch, Kingston Penitentiary Hospital Patient's Diaries, RG 73, Acc 87-88/014, Series III, Box 20A, Page 55, Library and Archives Canada.

The key prison officers were the warden, deputy warden, physician, and chaplain. They were all appointed by the government. But the rules and regulations of the prison were decided by a Board of Inspectors, voluntary positions held by local "worthies" appointed by government.[66]

The warden was the business manager (keeping prisoners employed, making contracts to sell their labour, purchasing supplies, keeping accounts); the deputy warden was in charge of discipline. The day to day supervision was handled by keepers and guards.[67]

As Kingston Penitentiary operated only in the final few years of the Upper Canada period, on which this guide focuses, I will not attempt to describe the challenges it faced during its history except to say that the first fifteen years were really brutal. Lack of funding meant poor quality, often rotten food, and discipline was extremely harsh. Despite the rosy predictions, convict labour never brought in nearly enough wages to pay the expenses of the prison. And it seems that too much power led to many abuses by prison staff.[68]

Punishment Records

Note: This inventory only contains records that begin before 1841. Many other records will be available for the post-1841 period.

Conviction Returns

Conviction returns were submitted by the relevant magistrates to the Clerks of the Peace, who then created master conviction registers, including:

- the names of the prosecutor, defendant, and presiding justice or magistrate;
- the charge;
- the date and sentence of the conviction;
- the amount of the fine (if any), when it is to be paid, and to whom; and
- if it wasn't paid, the rationale for non-payment.

Very few pre-1841 conviction returns have survived. These are the ones I've discovered:

Inventory

- AO RG 22-112 Western District (Windsor) Court of General Quarter Sessions of Peace, convictions

1835–1864 in Hiram Walker Collection, MS 205.

- PCMA Peterborough County Court fonds, 1830–1909: includes convictions.
- TUA 90-005 Victoria County fonds, 1834–1969: General Quarter Sessions of the Peace, includes convictions.
- TUA United Counties of Northumberland and Durham. Court records fonds, 1803–1955: General Quarter Sessions of the Peace, includes conviction returns, magistrate's returns.

Gaol Records

Two types of records are commonly found: registers and calendars. A register is an ongoing record that keeps track of each prisoner as he or she is committed. A calendar is a snapshot of the gaol population at a particular moment or period in time. These are usually produced for each quarter year. In some cases there are accompanying "dietary sheets" recording the food allowances provided to the prisoners.

Gaol registers often provide very detailed information about the prisoners they held. Generally, the information provided in gaol registers includes the name of the offender, the nature of the offence, the date admitted to gaol, and the release date. Other information can also be found in the records of specific gaols and for specific years. For example, the Gore District criminal register also recorded national origin, age, and gender for each offender for the years 1832 to 1851; occupations from 1843 to 1847; literacy from 1848 to 1851; and moral habits from 1848 to 1851.[69]

Though not included in this inventory, you may also find records of gaol tenders (people approved to supply goods or services to the gaol), and documents relating to the design and construction of gaols.

Note: although the Archives of Ontario uses the modern term "jail" to describe its records, the original records generally use the term "gaol."

Inventory

- AO RG 20-66 Administrative Records of the Cobourg (Newcastle District) Jail, 1834–1975, MS 2720.
- AO RG 20-70 Guelph Jail register, 1840–1977.
- AO RG 20-72 Hamilton (Gore District) Jail Records, 1832–1975, MS 454. These include jail registers, committal warrants.
- AO RG 20-100 Toronto (Home District) Jail Records, 1837–1975, MS 2782.
- AO RG 22-43 Newcastle District (Cobourg) Jail Records (calendars and medical reports), 1820–1846.
- AO RG 22-1894 Western District (Windsor) Jail calendars, 1821–1857.
- AO RG 22-2843 Lanark County (Perth) Jail Records, 1837–1863.
- AO RG 40-70 Wellington County (Guelph) Jail Records, 1840–1977, MS 2747.
- LAC RG 5 B27 Upper Canada and Canada West: Civil and Provincial Secretaries. Include gaol calendars and prison returns by district, 1823–1847, 4 volumes.
- TPL S278 Toronto Jail Statistical Registers

  - Register of Prisoners, 1838–1853, just a list of names.
  - Register of Prisoners, 1849–1852, details of committal, crime, etc.

- Register of Prisoners, 1874–1877, details of committal, crime, etc.

- TPL L16 William Dummer Powell papers, B87: Papers regarding prisoners and trials throughout Upper Canada, 1794–1825. Mostly calendars of prisoners.
- "Index to Gore District Debtors and Creditors, 1832–1849," *www.uppercanadagenealogy.com*. Index of the names of residents of Gore District who were gaoled for unpaid debts and the people to whom they owed money.
- "Index of Cobourg Jail Inmates, 1832–1848," *www.ontariogenealogy.com/cobourgcriminal.html*.

Grand Jury Presentments

These inspection reports describe the state of the gaol, sometimes commenting on specific prisoners. Where they are not specifically identified, they can often be found among the Quarter Sessions filings.

Inventory

- AO RG 22-38 Newcastle District (Cobourg) Court of General Quarter Sessions of Peace, grand jury presentments, 1822–1841.
- AO RG 22-106 Western District (Windsor) Court of General Quarter Sessions of Peace, grand jury presentments, 1794–1874, MS 166.
- UWO B155 London District Quarter Sessions Records

  - Reports of the Grand Jury on the state of the London District Gaol, 1831, 1834, 1835.

- Report of the Gaol Committee on the London District Gaol, 1834.

Penitentiary Records

Records of Kingston Penitentiary, which opened in 1835, are sparse for the first few years, but become voluminous as time goes on. Relevant records for the Upper Canada period are listed below.

Inventory

- LAC RG 13 D1 Operational Records of the Penitentiary Branch, 1834–1962. Files on escapes, transfers, convictions, and sentences of prisoners at federal institutions.
- LAC RG 73 Kingston Penitentiary Registers, 1835–1974, T1943-T2029. The records consist of microfilm copies of: punishment books, medical registers, warden journals, warden letterbooks, inspector's letterbooks, duty rosters, liberation books, and related material.
- "Hugh Armstrong's List of Convict Deaths at Kingston Penitentiary, 1835–1915," *www.cangenealogy.com/armstrong/kpart.htm*.

Registers of Fines and Estreats

When a person's sentence involved payment of a fine or court costs, records can be found among the accounts of the court, as well as in separate lists of fines and estreats. Estreats are a record of fines and recognizances that were imposed on an accused by the

Court of General Sessions of the Peace, which had subsequently become forfeit to the Crown. For example, in the case of recognizances, an accused would forfeit the £10 of his recognizance if he failed to perform the obligation (usually to appear in court) specified in his recognizance.

Inventory

- LAC RG5 B29 Clerks of the Peace, Extracts of Fines, 1811–1833, files for each District.
- AO RG 22-16 Johnstown District (Brockville) Court of General Quarter Sessions of Peace, Accounts, 1796–1845.
- AO RG 22-34 Newcastle District (Cobourg) Court of General Quarter Sessions of Peace, accounts, 1801–1848.
- AO RG 22-105 Western District (Windsor) Court of General Quarter Sessions of Peace, accounts, 1833–1842, MS 166.
- AO RG 22-111 Western District (Windsor) Court of General Quarter Sessions of Peace, accounts, 1818–1869 in Hiram Walker Collection, MS 205.
- AO RG 22-19 Johnstown District (Cornwall) Court of General Quarter Sessions of the Peace Estreats, 1803–1837.
- AO RG 22-41 Newcastle District (Cobourg) Court of General Quarter Sessions of the Peace Estreats, 1837–1847, organized chronologically by year, also found mixed in with the general records of the courts of quarter sessions.
- AO RG 22-63 London District (London) Court of General Quarter Sessions of the Peace Estreats, 1821–1831.
- AO RG 22-97 York County (York/Toronto) Court of General Quarter Sessions of Peace, estreats, 1800–1845, MS 251.

- AO RG 22-766: Estreats and Miscellaneous Register, 1807–1817. Series consists of a register that was kept by the Crown Office for the Court of King's Bench. The register contains several sections, mostly relating to estreats.

Newspaper Reports of Convictions

Reports of convictions and sentences often appeared in local newspapers following the conclusion of the court session. These are sometimes the only surviving records.

CHAPTER FIVE

Public Opinion:
Popular Response and Resistance

Newspaper Reports

Upper Canada may have been sparsely settled and rudimentary in its judicial processes, but it was extremely well served by the press. Over fifty newspapers were published during that period. Some lasted for only a few issues but others had impressive runs, such as the *Niagara Herald*, which began in 1801 and was still being published in 1886. The earliest was the *Upper Canada Gazette*. It began in 1793 and ran until 1845. Major towns and cities, such as York, Niagara, and Kingston, supported several newspapers at once, each with its own political point of view.

Notices of upcoming court sessions were frequently printed to allow people to plan to attend and reports of the convictions from each session were a regular feature. Some individual cases were reported in great detail, especially if they involved local notables, or particularly serious crimes.

Newspaper reports are often available when the official court records are missing, and frequently the newspapers reported far more detail than the official records. However, they were far from

Assize Report,
Kingston Gazette, *9
September 1817.*

KINGSTON, SEPTEMBER 9, 1817.

The Court of ASSIZE for the Midland District, commenced in this town on Monday, the 1st instant, and rose yesterday, about 1 o'clock —his Honor Chief Justice POWELL, presiding.

The following criminals were tried and convicted, viz,

WILLIAM STEEL and DANIEL CARTY, convicted of *Sheep-Stealing*—sentenced to be publickly whipped in the Market Place, once a week, for three successive weeks.

WILLIAM CLARK, convicted of *Grand Larceny*—sentenced to be whipped at any period within one month, at the discretion of the Sheriff with respect to time and place.

JOEL H. STODDARD, convicted of *Horse Stea'ing*—sentenced to be hanged.

SALLY BRADLEY, alias SMITH, convicted of *Petit Larceny*—sentenced to be confined 14 days in the prison, and at the expiration of that time, to be privately whipped within the gaol.

JOHN McDONELL, convicted of *Grand Larceny*—sentenced to be confined one month in the prison, and at the expiration of that time, to be publickly whipped in the Market Place.

MARY AIRHART, convicted of *Manslaughter,* prayed benefit of Clergy—sentenced to solitary confinement for six months, and to pay one shilling fine to the King.

TIMOTHY MAGINNIS, who was charged with the murder of Thomas Jackson, was acquitted by the Grand Jury, and discharged in Court.

MOST ATROCIOUS MURDERS !!

Several most atrocious murders were lately committed in the London District, Townsend, near the "Round Plains," A mother and six children were murdered by some ruthless hand—suspicion says the father of the family. His name is Henry Sovereign.— He had eleven children—three of them being of age, left home to procure a livelihood elsewhere, and one escaped the murderous havoc by being overlooked while asleep in the bed. Sovereign was committed to jail on suspicion, and he behaved so obstinately and disorderly on the way thither, that the Constable and Sheriff were obliged to stop and get handcuffs made and put on him. The following particulars respecting these dreadful murders have been communicated by the Rev. William Ryerson, who lately visited the London District, and was an eye witness of some of the facts stated.

"Most Atrocious Murders!" Christian Guardian, *1 February 1832.*

impartial. Each newspaper had its own political affiliation, and the editors had a great deal of control over what got printed and how events were described. Where possible, it's important to check all the newspapers for the area. For example, the trial and execution of William Brass for rape in 1837 (defended by a young John A. MacDonald — his first major case), was reported in at least three Kingston newspapers: the *British Whig*, the *Chronicle and Gazette*, and the *Upper Canada Herald*.

The *British Whig* devoted nearly 2,000 words to the trial, including providing a brief biography of the accused and his family, and describing the judge's address to the jury, the testimony of each witness, including questions posed on cross-examination, and the final arguments. The editors were clearly sympathetic to the prisoner and his family. They had reported in detail on an earlier dispute in which Brass was the victim of a fraud by a disreputable lawyer. They also made a point of praising the judge for his clear and impartial handling of the case and Brass's lawyer, John A. MacDonald, for his "very able defence."[1]

The day of Brass's execution, the *Whig* again reported in great detail, and that time editorial comment was not held back. The execution went horribly wrong when the drop failed to operate properly and the rope was too long. Brass had to be taken up the stairs again and dropped a second time. The *Whig* called upon the sheriff to explain his apparent negligence and reported verbatim part of Brass's lengthy speech prior to his execution.[2]

The *Upper Canada Herald* gave a somewhat shorter account of the trial, summarizing the testimony of each witness rather than going into all the details. There was very little editorial comment in the *Herald's* report, other than to note that the Solicitor General prosecuted the case "with great moderation towards the prisoner."[3]

The *Chronicle and Gazette* provided a very brief summary of the trial, but took pains to point out the "ingenious" defence by Mr. MacDonald and the impartiality of the solicitor general's prosecution. The *Chronicle's* report of the execution was extremely brief, but they supported the sheriff against his critics, calling him "worthy" and chastising those who accused him of "inhumanity or brutality of conduct."[4]

Petitions and Appeals

The justice system was theoretically dedicated to the service of the people, but the "public" didn't always agree with the decisions of the court. Since prior to 1849 there was no appeal court, the only recourse was to appeal to the Lieutenant-Governor. Private citizens frequently decided to petition the Lieutenant-Governor for mercy

Petition regarding Caleb Wilson alias Swayze, 18 October 1816, Upper Canada Sundries, Library and Archives Canada, RG 5 A1 Volume 30, 13,754–57.

for themselves and their friends, relatives, and neighbours. This was particularly common in response to sentences of execution, but also frequent for shaming sentences such as whipping and the stocks and pillory. A large number of those requests were granted. In fact, judges were required to report directly to the Lieutenant-Governor following each Assize, describing each of the capital convictions, and indicating where there were sufficient grounds for mercy.[5]

For example, a group of seventy-three residents of the Niagara District wrote to Lieutenant-Governor Gore to petition for clemency for a seventeen-year-old boy named Caleb Wilson (alias Swayze) who, on 18 October 1816, had been convicted of horse stealing and sentenced to death by hanging.

As was common practice in the early days, when paper was expensive, the decision of the Lieutenant-Governor was written on the reverse of the petition. It read: "The sentence commuted to perpetual banishment, 19 October 1816." So the petition of his friends and neighbours was successful, and young Caleb escaped the noose.

For less serious offences, petitions might be addressed to the district magistrates. These can be found among the records of the Quarter Sessions of the Peace.

Resistance

Representatives of the law, such as magistrates, sheriffs, and constables, were often resented by the local population. Some of those feelings were due to the harsh debt laws of the time, which allowed a farmer's land to be seized by the sheriff and auctioned off when the farmer got too far behind in his lease or mortgage payments.[6] People sometimes fought back by resisting arrest, appealing convictions, and filing law suits against constables and magistrates for exceeding their powers, neglecting their duty or misconduct.[7]

For example, Susan Lewthwaithe describes a complex series of events that took place in the rural township of Burford in 1839, in her article: "Violence, Law, and Community in Rural Upper Canada."[8] The trouble began when John Thomson, a new arrival to the area, purchased a farm from William Cruden. Thomson paid Cruden in cash and Cruden was supposed to give him back $46 in change. When Cruden didn't give Thomson the change, Cruden took him to civil court for it. Also, Thomson had agreed to let Cruden use an old log house on the property to store his livestock crops until he could sell them. But after the agreed upon six weeks had passed, Cruden moved his belongings to a barn on the property and wouldn't remove them. Cruden and his friends started harassing Thomson and damaging his property. Thomson's testimony even accused them of threatening his life.

Thomson went to a local magistrate, John Weir, to ask for help in dealing with his neighbour. Weir tried to get Thomson to settle his differences with Cruden using independent arbitration rather than formal charges, but Thomson wanted Weir to do something right away. Weir issued a peace bond against Cruden and his wife, but it didn't stop the harassment. Finally, one day Thomson went to Weir to complain that one of Cruden's friends, Allan Muir, had broken through his gate and damaged his fence. Weir wrote up a warrant for the arrest of Muir and gave it to his son Robert to take to the local constable. When Robert Weir couldn't find the constable (he wasn't home), another magistrate, George Whitehead, told him to go ahead and execute the warrant himself since Robert was a "special constable." They found Allan Muir at William Cruden's house, along with three other men armed with knives they'd been using to slaughter pigs. Cruden and the other men tried to prevent the arrest, and were extremely insulting towards both Robert and John Weir (who had followed his son), but Robert Weir finally got Muir out of the house and started taking him toward the local inn, several miles away, where the magistrates had arranged to try his case the next day.

Robert Weir rode his horse, John Weir was in a sleigh, but Muir was made to walk. In order to prevent Muir from escaping, John Weir told Robert to tie Muir to the horse with a rope. Muir would later claim that he had protested that he had a bad knee and couldn't walk that far, but the Weirs wouldn't let him ride and, in fact, half-dragged him for at least a quarter of a mile. The next day, John Weir and two other magistrates convicted Muir of trespassing and levied a fine (amount unrecorded, but under £5 as this was the upper limit for summary convictions).

That wasn't the end of the story, for Muir, Cruden, and their friends had long-standing grievances against John Weir, many of which probably boiled down to political differences; the Weirs were staunch Tories and the Muir and his friends (and most Burford residents) were radical Reformers.

Muir appealed the conviction at the next sitting of the Court of Quarter Sessions and it was overturned (it seems that this was because the jury decided that Robert Weir had not shown the arrest warrant to Muir, so the arrest was illegal). Muir also brought a civil action against the Weirs for trespass, assault, and false imprisonment, which was taken to the higher court. In the meantime, William Cruden had written to the Lieutenant-Governor complaining about John Weir, accusing him of being a tyrant, of overstepping his authority, misappropriating the fines he collected, and of generally having bad character since he had been seen frequenting places of public entertainment. Cruden had gathered a petition against Weir with the signatures of 240 residents. The testimony concerning what exactly happened during the arrest was highly contradictory, but the jury believed Muir and his witnesses, and found for the plaintiff. John Weir was ordered to pay £16 in damages to Allan Muir.

The Chief Justice's report included the following statement: "I explained to the Jury that where a Magistrate is called upon to act in a remote country place, against such lawless characters as the two Muirs were stated to be, it is his duty not to suffer his authority to be treated with contempt, and the law to be overborne; because if he were remiss in that respect, his fellow subjects should not receive that protection in their persons and property which the law gives them a right to look for."[9]

Extra-Legal Solutions

Finally, sometimes people preferred to take the law into their own hands. There are reports of the use of the "charivari," an ancient European tradition, in Upper Canada. This was basically a form of social censure for behaviour the community disapproves of.

One example took place in Ancaster Township in 1826. George Rolph was the Clerk of the Peace for the Gore District, as well as registrar of the surrogate court and clerk of the district (civil) court. He had been appointed in 1816 and gained a reputation for snobbery because he chose not to live in either of the towns of Dundas or Ancaster, where the wealthy and powerful resided, and he did not attend the parties and social events expected of someone of his position. He also supported the cause of political reform, which pitted him against the sheriff, most of the magistrates, and the ruling elite. For these reasons, he was not well-liked among the elite of the district, but they had nothing concrete to criticize until he hired a married woman, Mrs. Evans, as his housekeeper and she and her young child moved into his home. Rolph was married, and Mrs. Evans had left her husband. Rolph and Evans were suspected of having an affair.

One night a group of men with blackened faces broke into his house, dragged Rolph out of his bed (in which Mrs. Evans was not sleeping), stripped him, beat him, smeared him with tar, and covered him with feathers, all the while threatening him with further injury saying they would "cut [him] in a way too horrible to describe."[10] They left him alone and half-conscious on the ground outside his house.

When Rolph finally identified a few of the perpetrators (the sheriff, his son-in-law, and a prominent physician), he sued them for damages. In court, the defence lawyer, Henry John Boulton (who was solicitor general at the time and would have had to prosecute the case if it were a criminal one), did not even try to claim that the plaintiffs hadn't attacked Rolph, but instead argued, "In this country where there is no other punishment for so gross a breach of public morals and public decency than public opinion and public rebuke, the men who stood forward to vindicate the rights of an outraged community deserved rather praise than punishment."[11] The jury found for Rolph, but the damages the magistrates imposed were extremely lenient under the circumstances (£20 each — the prosecution had asked for £1000).

The Rolph incident was a one-time event perpetrated by a group of outraged individuals, but in some parts of Upper Canada vigilante gangs operated on a regular basis. One such gang was known as the Cavan Blazers.

George Berry, an early settler in Durham County, recounted his recollections of the activities of the Blazers, as follows:

> The Cavan Blazers were the social regulators of
> the early days in the northern part of Durham ...
> Now-a-days it is all law, law, law. If any little dis-
> pute occurs between neighbours, or if someone
> is acting in a manner injurious to the community,
> the magistrate and constable must be called in.
> "The Blazers" settled all such matters in the early
> days without delay, without cost, and with less
> of ill-feeling than follows upon legal proceedings
> now. Not only that, but they made the punish-
> ment fit the crime in the case of men whose
> offences could not be reached in the ordinary
> way....Then there was a postmaster who insisted

on pasturing his calf on the roadway. A nearby church and adjoining cemetery were both open to the road, and the calf would go into the grave-yard and feed on the long grass. Then, as a chill came on with the night, it would lie on the warm steps of the church and leave them in a most filthy state by morning. "The Blazers" stood it as long as possible, and then one Saturday night something happened. When the store-keeper got up late Sunday morning, he found the calf boxed up in a large crockery crate in front of his store door and the crate securely anchored with some heavy stones and a block of timber placed on top. The lesson was effective. There was no more desecration of the place of burial and the church steps no longer required scrubbing every Sunday morning before service.[12]

Public Opinion Records

Note: This inventory only contains records that begin before 1841. Many other records will be available for the post-1841 period.

Petitions and Appeals

When people disagreed with a sentence, or wanted to appeal for mercy, they wrote to the relevant authority. Fortunately, these records are very well kept. Unfortunately, they are so voluminous that they are difficult to locate without an index.

Inventory

- LAC RG 5 A1 Civil secretary, correspondence (incoming) also known as the Upper Canada Sundries (an index to criminal matters appearing in these records has been published in Talbot's *Justice in Early Ontario*; see below).
- LAC RG 5 A2 Civil secretary, correspondence (outgoing), drafts of replies.
- LAC RG 7 G16 Civil secretary, correspondence (outgoing), replies sent.
- LAC R188-36-2-E (formerly RG 13-F-1) Department of Justice fonds, Office of the Attorney General of Canada West, 1800–1866. Series consists of correspondence, authorizations, and legal documents relating to matters under the supervision of the attorney general of Canada West and his predecessor the attorney general of Upper Canada. These papers include a large number of memorials and petitions.
- LAC RG 68 Registrar General: Warrants and Pardons. Include various records relating to warrants for the removal of prisoners and some pardons, 1818–1953. Most of the records are available on microfilm.
- TPL L16 William Dummer Powell papers. B94: Warrants for (six) pardons issued by Lieutenant-Governor Maitland, 1820–1823.
- Talbot, Charles K. *Justice in Early Ontario, 1791–1840.* Ottawa: Crimcare Publications, 1983.

Resistance

Records of resistance to authorities will be found among the investigative and adjudication records described above, assuming the resisters were every charged with an office.

Extra-Legal Solutions

Records of vigilantes will be found among the investigative and adjudication records described above, assuming they were ever charged with an office.

CHAPTER SIX

Justice Personnel

Officers of the Crown

The key justice officials in Upper Canada were the attorney general, solicitor general, judges, sheriffs, and magistrates, all of whom were appointed directly by the Lieutenant-Governor. There were few criteria for the jobs. In fact, they weren't even treated as employment, but more like titles or a form of property (as they came with significant fees and privileges and they were generally for life, barring gross incompetence). Appointments to government offices were a form of political patronage, a way of rewarding people for their loyalty. Competency, knowledge, or experience were generally not required. Rather, appointments went to people who could be counted upon to be loyal to the Crown in general and their superiors in particular.[1]

Attorney General and Solicitor General

At the top of the legal hierarchy were the Attorney General and Solicitor General, both of whom were appointed by the British Colonial Office "at pleasure," which generally meant for life, unless promoted or dismissed for extreme incompetence. The Attorney General was responsible for providing legal advice to the members of the Executive Council and the Lieutenant-Governor, and prosecuting serious criminal cases on behalf of the Crown at the Assizes.[2]

The Solicitor General shared these responsibilities as a kind of understudy or assistant and almost always became Attorney General when the position became vacant. Informally, these positions were considered "training grounds" for judicial positions on the Court of King's Bench.[3] In addition to their official duties, most Attorneys General also maintained private law practices, as in the early years their roles were not onerous.[4]

They received an annual salary (the Attorney General £300, the Solicitor General £100), as well as a monopoly on the provision of certain legal services, for which they charged fees, such as prosecutions and approving government legal documents, e.g., land grant fiats and commissions of appointment for other offices.[5]

The Attorneys General during the Upper Canada years were, in order: John White, Thomas Scott, William Firth, J. McDonell, D'Arcy Boulton, John Beverley Robinson, Henry John Boulton.[6]

The Solicitors General during the Upper Canada years were, in order: Robert Isaac Dey Gray, D'Arcy Boulton, John Beverley Robinson, Henry John Boulton, and Christopher Hagerman.[7]

D'Arcy Boulton served as Solicitor General of Upper Canada from 1805 to 1813 and Attorney General from 1814 to 1818. Born in 1759, he was the son of a wealthy Lincolnshire barrister. Arriving in Upper Canada in 1802, after a few years in New York, he first settled in the township of Augusta (near Cornwall). He was almost immediately placed on the books of the Upper Canada Law Society as a barrister-at-law, even though he had no formal training. In 1807 he moved to York (later Toronto), the capital of Upper Canada, where he quickly became a key member of the Tory establishment. In fact, his name later became synonymous with the "Family Compact." In 1810, while en route to England, his boat was attacked by a French privateer. Although he led the passengers in a "stout" defence, they were taken prisoner and he spent the next four years in prison in Verdun. Upon his return to Upper Canada in 1814, Boulton was hailed as a hero and promoted to Attorney General. In that role, he was involved in the famous trials of Paul Brown and F. F. Bourcher, who were accused of the murder of Robert Semple in "Red River Country" in 1816. In 1818 Boulton was again promoted, that time to the Court of King's Bench, where he remained until illness forced him to retire in 1827.[8]

Judges of the Court King's Bench

The Court of King's Bench was the highest court in Upper Canada. At first it consisted of the Chief Justice and two Puisne[9] Justices. In 1837, it was expanded to five judges (and then reduced back to three in 1849).[10] As with all other government appointments, the early ones were "short on judicial experience and long on patronage."[11]

The Chief Justice was second only to the Lieutenant-Governor in power and prestige. His annual salary reflected that position, at £1,000 in 1791.[12]

There were only seven Chief Justices during the Upper Canada period. Their names, with years of appointment, were: William Osgoode (1792), John Elmsley (1796), Henry Allcock (1802), Thomas Scott (1806), William Dummer Powell (1816), William Campbell (1825), and John Beverley Robinson (1829).[13]

William Dummer Powell, *C. W. Jefferys*, The Picture Gallery of Canadian History, *Volume 2, 68.*

William Dummer Powell
Judge Court of King's Bench

The Puisne Judges were: William Dummer Powell (1794), Peter Russell (1794), Henry Allcock (1798), Thomas Cochrane (1803), Robert Thorpe (1805), William Campbell (1811), D'Arcy Boulton (1818), Levius Peters Sherwood (1825), James Buchanan Macaulay (1827), John Walpole Willis (1827), and Christopher Alexander Hagerman (1828).[14]

William Dummer Powell, who served as Chief Justice from 1816 to 1825, was the first incumbent who had actual experience as a judge. He had been a magistrate in the Hesse District (Western) since 1789, and then served a Puisne Judge of the Court of King's Bench until his promotion to Chief Justice.[15] He was born in 1755, in Boston, Massachusetts, to a prominent Royalist family. In 1775, he and his wife left the United States just as the Revolution was about to begin, and moved to Britain. In Britain, he began training in the law. A few years later he emigrated to Canada, arriving in Quebec in 1779, where he obtained a licence to practice law and went into private practice in Montreal. His position as a the first judge of common pleas at Detroit was a prestigious one, as Detroit was a fur-trading centre, and the court had jurisdiction well beyond the district in order to enforce its control of this commercial activity. However, his American connections made it difficult for him to be quickly accepted in British circles. Powell coveted the position of Chief Justice from the start, but had to wait many years for that dream to become reality. In 1808 he was appointed to the Executive Council and moved to York (Toronto), where he lived the rest of this life. As Chief Justice, Powell was known for his insistence on the letter of the law, to the point of using one hundred-year-old technicalities. He retired from both the Executive Council and the bench in 1825, at the age of seventy, living another nine years in retirement. He and his wife were prominent members of the local aristocracy. [16]

Justices of the Peace (Also Called Magistrates)

Each district was administered by a local magistracy composed of Justices of the Peace, appointed by the Lieutenant-Governor (often virtually for life). Collectively the Justices of the Peace formed both the Court of General Quarter Sessions of the Peace and the local government.[17] They set tax rates, paid salaries, appointed other district officials, issued licences of all kinds, administered the swearing of oaths, authorized the building and repair of roads and bridges, and looked after social welfare.[18] During the cholera epidemic of 1832, the magistrates were ordered to form a board of health to oversee quarantines and medical care. They also conducted preliminary investigations in criminal cases, and sometimes acted as coroners where there was none available.[19]

Magistrates Appointed for the Johnstown District, 1837–1840, Magistrates Book, Archives of Ontario, RG 8-15, Volume 1.

The only qualification for the job was an income of £100 year.[20] Presumably, that guaranteed that magistrates were solid, respectable citizens who could be relied upon to be loyal to the government. Nepotism was taken for granted as sitting magistrates were frequently asked to make recommendations for new appointments.[21]

Most Justices of the Peace had no legal training.[22] They often served in multiple public offices as well as having private interests (many were merchants), since the role did not require a full-time commitment. The only restriction was that you couldn't be sheriff and magistrate at the same time.[23]

Each district might have dozens of magistrates. The intent was to make sure they were accessible to everyone. However, many magistrates weren't very active most of the time. For example, of the 117 justices named in the commissions of the Peace for Niagara District in 1833, only six to twenty showed up for each Quarter Session.[24]

Magistrates weren't paid salaries. Their remuneration came from fees, and even then they didn't get much. It was a position of power, not wealth.[25] Legislation in 1834 standardized the fees payable across the province. They could bill 10s. for each record of conviction they prepared; 7s. 6d. for every conviction they made under a penal statute; 2s. and 6d. for each recognizance, warrant, certificate of dismissal, and summary conviction they issued; 3s. 9d. for information and each warrant for apprehension for assault or other misdemeanor they prepared; 1s. and 3d. for every other information or discharge they prepared; and 6d. for each subpoena they issued.[26]

Mahlon Burwell is an excellent example of the power of patronage appointments in Upper Canada. Born in New Jersey in 1783 to a Loyalist family, he grew up in Bertie Township in the Niagara District. He had very minimal schooling (less than a year), but took up the profession of surveying, and with the support of Thomas Talbot was hired by the provincial government to lay out many of the roads and townships in southwestern Ontario. He served as a lieutenant-colonel in the militia during the War of 1812. He built Trinity (Anglican) Church in Port Burwell, and formed a company there to promote harbour development and the shipment of timber. In 1809 he was appointed to the lucrative post of registrar of lands for Middlesex County and in 1812 he was elected to the House of Assembly, serving until 1824 and again from 1830 to 1834. In 1813 he was commissioned Justice of the Peace. In 1820 he was also commissioned collector of customs at Port Talbot. In 1824, he was appointed coroner for London District. By 1828, he virtually controlled all of the civil and military appointments within Middlesex County.[27]

Clerks of the Peace

Each district had a Clerk of the Peace appointed by the Lieutenant-Governor. The clerk's role was to assist the magistrates by creating and keeping the records of the court and local government. Their judicial duties included keeping minutes of the Quarter Sessions, drawing indictments, issuing warrants and summons, making up annual lists of inhabitant householders eligible for jury duty and delivering it to the sheriff; filing Justice of the Peace's Returns of Convictions and Returns of Fines, Penalties and so on; publishing the returns in the newspaper of the district; and recording the place and time of sittings of the court.

During the Upper Canada period, most Clerks of the Peace had no legal training, but they did have to be relatively well educated.[28] Like magistrates, Clerks of the Peace were not paid salaries, but earned their income by charging fees for specific services such as preparing summons, making copies of judgments, and creating reports.

In 1819, the Clerks of the Peace were:[29]

- Ottawa District: Peter Leroy
- Eastern District: George Anderson
- Johnstown District: T.D. Campbell
- Midland District: Alexander Pringle
- Newcastle District: Eleas Jones
- Home District: Stephen Howard
- Gore District: George Rolph
- Niagara District: J.B. Clench
- London District: R.W. Dease
- Western District: G.T.F. Ireland

George Rolph was Clerk of the Peace for the Gore District from 1816 (at the age of twenty-two) to 1829. He was somewhat unusual, as he held several prominent government positions despite being a committed reformer. His brother, John Rolph, was one of the most well-known reformers in Upper Canada. George Rolph had little legal training prior to his appointment as Clerk of the Peace (as well as Clerk of the District Court and Clerk of the Surrogate Court), but he did have an extensive liberal education, which was the main prerequisite for a legal career in Upper Canada. He was born in England in 1782, and moved to Upper Canada with his parents when he was a teenager. He served in the War of 1812 as a lieutenant, participating in the Battle of Queenston Heights. In 1828, he was elected to the Legislative Assembly representing Halton County (he served only until 1830). Following a scandal in which Rolph was accused of having an affair with a married woman, he was forced out of the position of Clerk of the Peace for the Quarter Sessions. However, he continued to serve the Clerk of the Surrogate Court for many years (fifty-four in all). He died in 1875 at the age of eighty-one.[30]

Account of Alpheus St. John, Coroner, Lincoln County Court of General Sessions of the Peace Records, 1836, Archives of Ontario, RG 22-372, Box 25, Folder 1.

Coroners

Appointed by the Lieutenant-Governor, coroners had the same authority as Justices of the Peace. They could hear testimony from witnesses, call on medical personnel for their opinions, and gather whatever other evidence they required. They could then call a coroner's jury to examine the evidence and make a verdict concerning a cause of death or the cause of a fire. Most early coroners had very little, if any, medical or legal training.

The role of coroner was not a full-time responsibility, thus they had no salary. They were paid only when their services were required to investigate a death or fire.

Sheriffs

Each district had a sheriff, appointed at pleasure by the Lieutenant-Governor. It was a coveted and lucrative office.[31] The annual salary of most sheriffs in those days was £50, so the bulk of their income would come from fees charged for specific services.[32] For example, in the Ottawa District in 1821 the sheriff's income from fees was £100, while in the Niagara District in 1833 the sheriff's income from fees was £1,200.[33]

The role of the sheriff was to carry out the processes mandated by the courts. That involved making arrests, keeping the gaol (jail), executing sentences — including hangings, summoning jurors for jury duty, attending the Quarter Sessions, seizing and selling property forfeited under judgment of debt, and maintaining general order in the county courthouse.[34]

The sheriff was also expected to support the government in all ways. That was illustrated by the dismissal of Thomas Merritt, who had served ably as sheriff of the Niagara District for seventeen years before Lieutenant-Governor Maitland fired him in 1820 for allowing (allegedly even assisting) a political radical (Robert Gourlay) to publish seditious articles in the local newspaper while confined in the Niagara gaol.[35]

Sheriffs were asked for recommendations for suitable candidates for commissions of Justices of the Peace and other local government offices, and were also expected to be the "eyes and ears" of the government in their districts, informing the Lieutenant-Governor of suspicious activities and characters.[36]

> While walking to church on a Sunday with the postmaster and magistrate at Fort Erie, James Kerby, in late April, 1827, Leonard [Sheriff Richard Leonard, of the Niagara District]

warned him that he was under suspicion for let-
ting William Mackenzie insert Kerby's name in
his paper as his agent. Kerby was so upset that he
immediately wrote to the lieutenant governor
with a full confession, pleading loyalty and deny-
ing any link to Mackenzie or to his politics.[37]

The sheriff's role could also be dangerous. There was popular
resentment around the seizure of property for things like unpaid
mortgage debts. Joseph Ryerson, sheriff of the London District,
was forced to resign the lucrative commission in fear for his life.
In October 1805 he wrote to the Lieutenant-Governor,

> Whilst I express my thanks and feelings of grati-
> tude towards the Executive government of this
> province for the honorable mark of distinc-
> tion bestowed upon me by appointing me to
> the office of sheriff of the district of London, I
> cannot but lament that the situation of the dis-
> trict compels me for my own safety to resign
> it and I pray your Honor to accept of this as
> my resignation of the said office. In doing it I
> beg your Honor to be assured that I have not
> been induced to take this step from any aversion
> to serve his Majesty or the country, but from
> a conviction that I cannot do it in the Office
> I now have the Honor of holding but at the
> imminent hazard of destruction to myself and
> family. I have therefore to request that your
> Honor will not consider me any longer Sheriff
> of the district of London.[38]

Justice Personnel

In 1821, the sheriffs of Upper Canada were:[39]

- Ottawa District: Thomas Mears
- Eastern District: Donald W. Donell
- Johnstown District: John Stuart
- Midland District: John McLean
- Newcastle District: John Spencer
- Home District: Samuel Ridout
- Gore District: Titus G. Simmons
- Niagara District: Richard Leonard
- London District: Abraham A. Rapelje
- Western District: William Hands

Henry Ruttan was sheriff of the Newcastle District for thirty years after being appointed in 1827. He is an excellent example of the lengthy periods for which early sheriffs served. He was born in 1792, the son of a United Empire Loyalist (as were many early office-holders). Prior to his appointment as sheriff, he had served in the Northumberland militia, joining to fight in the War of 1812 and achieving the rank of Colonel in 1825. He continued to serve in the active militia until 1846. In 1820, Ruttan was elected to the Legislative Assembly, serving until 1824 and then again from 1836 to 1841. His other activities included owning and operating a dry goods store in Grafton, inventing a system for heating and cooling railway coaches, and serving as president of the Provincial Agricultural Association. He lived a long and prosperous life, dying in Cobourg in 1871 at the age of seventy-nine.[40] Sheriff Ruttan attributed his successful career to an accident of fate. As a young child he lost two of his fingers to an axe. No longer fit for manual labour, his father sent him to school and the rest, as they say, was history.[41]

Sherrif Henry Ruttan, *painting by Paul Kane, c. 1835. Library and Archives Canada, C-147925.*

Gaolors, Turnkeys, Wardens, Guards

Not much has been written about the role of the gaoler (aka jailer) and related occupations, despite them being among the few positions in the justice system that were full-time. In fact, gaolers and turnkeys (assistants) were often on duty twenty-four hours a day.[42]

For this burdensome responsibility, gaolers were not highly paid (although rates varied from district to district). For example, in 1817 the Home District gaolor received £70, which also had to pay his turnkey/assistant. In 1837 he got £200 (paying £30 to £50 for each turnkey).[43]

Debtors confined to gaol often complained of the conditions under which they were held and about their lawyers not helping them, but they didn't seem to complain about the gaolers. Presumably, they believed they were treated as fairly as possible under the circumstances.[44] Despite their thankless job, it seems as though the gaolers were doing the best they could under difficult circumstances.

• • •

During the Upper Canada period the only prison was Kingston Penitentiary, which opened in 1835. That institution was run by the warden and deputy warden, who were appointed by the legislature.[45]

The warden was the business manager. His responsibilities included keeping the prisoners employed, making contracts to sell their labour, purchasing supplies, and keeping accounts. The deputy warden was in charge of disciplining the prisoners.[46] The day-to-day supervision of the prisoners was handled by keepers and guards.[47]

Constables

At least one constable was appointed annually for each township by the district magistrates sitting as the Court of Quarter Sessions of the Peace. By the 1830s some townships were electing their

Account of Walter Willson, Turnkey, Lincoln County Court of General Sessions of the Peace Records, 1836, Archives of Ontario, RG 22-372, Box 25, Folder 1.

constables, who were then approved by the magistrates at the Court of Quarter Sessions.[48]

The only official criterion was that constables had to be British citizens. The magistrates generally looked for respectable but rugged men.[49] Exemptions included the very poor or ignorant; barristers, attorneys, and officers of Court of King's Bench;

List of Constables approved at the General Sessions, 1841, Lincoln County Court of General Sessions of the Peace Records, Archives of Ontario, RG 22-372, Box 41, Folder 23.

surgeons; and officers in the King's service. Gentlemen of quality and public-house keepers could apply for exemption to Court of King's Bench, if there were others able to serve.[50]

Aside from those who were exempted, no one could refuse the duty without penalty, but once a man had served for a year he could not be called up again for another three years.[51] The duty was intermittent — a constable had to be available to do whatever the magistrates needed him to do. But many constables were never called upon to act. In no way was constable an "occupation." They received no formal training or uniforms. Most constables were farmers, merchants, or otherwise engaged most of the time.[52]

Constables' duties were to assist the magistrates in enforcing the law when called upon, generally by serving subpoenas, executing search warrants, making arrests, and escorting prisoners to gaol.[53] Generally they did not act on their own authority, responding only when a magistrate summoned them. However, they were authorized to arrest "all traitors, felons and suspicious persons" and anyone the constables witnessed committing assault or treason, endangering life, or making violent threats.[54] They could also break into a house, if their entrance was denied, in order to "suppress disorderly drinking or noise at an unreasonable hour of the night."[55]

Constables were permitted to detain arrested persons until it was convenient to bring them before a magistrate. They could break open the doors of a house in order to make an arrest if peaceable entry was refused. And if a person who had committed a felony resisted arrest and tried to flee or escaped after being arrested, the constable was legally justified in killing him in cases of absolute necessity.[56]

If a constable needed help apprehending a criminal he could ask any people nearby to assist and they had to obey. He could also appoint a deputy to execute a warrant if he wasn't able to do it himself.[57]

Constables did not receive a salary. Instead they were paid for specific services and had their expenses covered after submitting their accounts to the Quarter Sessions.[58] For example, they could

Account of Donald McDonald, constable, Lincoln County Court of General Sessions of the peace Records, 1836, Archives of Ontario, RG 22-372, Box 25, Folder 1.

bill 4d. per mile for every mile they had to travel to execute a warrant, or serve a summons, and 8d. for every summons served.[59]

When constables were called upon, their role could be both difficult and dangerous. They often had to travel great distances in rotten weather to make arrests, deliver prisoners to gaol or court, and serve subpoenas on witnesses. En route, constables had to look after their prisoners at their own expense, for which they were later reimbursed. If the prisoner escaped in the night, sometimes the magistrates wouldn't approve their bills.[60] People often refused to respect the authority of the constables, and sometimes sued them for exceeding their powers, neglecting their duty, or misconduct. For example, in the Newcastle District between 1813 and 1840 there were at least fifty incidents (likely many more that weren't prosecuted) in which constables or bailiffs were assaulted or threatened.[61]

Donald McDonald's 1836 bill for services as a constable for the town of Niagara offers a peek into his duties. It records the following activities:

- Committing a man suspected of murder in Toronto and found in Buffalo.
- Looking after an orphan child for a night.
- Arresting a woman and four others for keeping a house of ill fame.
- Guarding the Niagara gaol for four nights prior to an execution.[62]

Despite the danger and low pay, most constables carried out their orders very well, receiving praise from the magistrates.[63] Of nearly 2,400 orders given to the Niagara constables by the magistrates or other legal officers, only six constables refused to carry out the order or otherwise acted inappropriately.[64]

Starting in 1817, the district magistrates were permitted to hire full-time "high constables" and part-time regular constables to serve in the newly created "police towns." These urban constables took on new responsibilities including those formerly assigned to bailiffs, such as inspecting chimneys and buildings for fire safety, monitoring the use of weights and measures in markets, controlling domestic animals within the town limits, and escorting inebriated men and women to their homes or the local gaol.[65]

As the towns grew, so did their need for manpower and formal organization. That was especially true in the Town of York (which became the City of Toronto in 1834). In 1810, the Town of York had eleven constables.[66] By 1823, there were twenty.[67]

With the incorporation of the City of Toronto came a new system of policing. A high constable was appointed and each alderman on the council had the right to appoint a constable in his ward. Not surprisingly, that led to many hard feelings and suggestions that the police force had become partisan and corrupt.[68] Ethnic divisions in the city were acerbated by the fact that the constables were all Orangemen (members of the Orange order, an Irish Protestant fraternal organization). When riots erupted in 1855 the constabulary took the side of the rioters against their victims, the newly arrived poor Roman Catholic Irish.[69] One critic noted, "In Toronto after the rebellion of 1837 the constabulary became virtually the legal auxiliary of militant Orangeism."[70]

The newly hired constables were paid 5s. a day for day duty and 7s. and 6d. for night duty.[71] In 1837, their pay was raised to a fixed rate of £75 per year.

William Higgins was appointed high constable for the Home District, a job that also included the duties of inspector of police for the Town of York (in charge of enforcing fire and sanitary regulations), in 1826.[72] Basically, his job was to watch over the town and protect the public from all risks to their welfare. His salary then was £40. When, in 1834, he was appointed high bailiff (including the duties of city inspector) for the newly incorporated City of Toronto, his salary was increased to £125. His new duties included those usually performed by the district sheriffs, such as selecting and summoning jurors to the Mayor's Court. He also remained high constable for the district. Clearly, Higgins was well respected, as his nomination was proposed by a Tory member of the council and unanimously approved by council, despite its domination by Reform members. However, an incident in 1835 put his reputation and career on the line.

During an election riot, in which Higgins and several constables were involved (ostensibly to keep the peace), a man named
Patrick Burns was killed. Several witnesses reported that Higgins
was closest to the man when he was stabbed, and that he had
said something like, "Burns, were you not a fool to resist me?"
However, after six days of conflicting testimony (including that
of over a dozen constables, who mostly supported Higgins), the
jury acquitted Higgins. Although he lost his position as high bailiff for the city, he remained high constable for the district (and
later for the County of York), and chief bailiff for the division
court until at least 1856. He also won a seat on city council in
1860, representing St. Lawrence Ward for three years.[73]

Juries

The third session of the Upper Canadian parliament (1794)
passed the Act to Establish Trials By Jury, which required all issues
of fact in all courts of law in Upper Canada to be "tried and
determined by the unanimous verdict of twelve jurors."

It was the responsibility of the sheriff to annually examine
the tax assessment rolls provided to him by the Clerk of the Peace
and make up two panels of eligible jurors: one for the grand jury,
which decided the validity of the case and the need for an indictment; and one for the petty (petit) juries, which considered the
evidence of each case and returned the verdict.[74] Most householders were eligible, but once a man had served on a jury he was
exempt for the next two years. Men over the age of sixty were also
exempt, as were Quakers, Mennonites, Moravians, and Tunkers
after 1809. Illness was also accepted as a temporary excuse.[75]

Petty Jurors 38 31

1 Antoine Bellperche of Maidstone Yeoman
2 Medard Petre " "
3 Constant Gautier " "
4 Joseph Bellemarche " "
5 Jean B. Arnout " "
6 Jean B. Petre " " Innkeeper
7 Jacob Miller " " Yeoman
8 Abner S. Henry " "
9 Pierre Charon " "
10 Jean Esperance " "
11 Charles Ouellette of Rochester Yeoman
12 Joseph Renaud ther " "
13 Joseph Renaud son " "
14 Andre Durocher " "
15 Louis Dutz " "
16 Antoine Knapp " "
17 Jean B. Durocher " "
18 Coleman Rowe of Raleigh Yeoman
19 Claude Cartier " Harwich Innkeeper
20 Michael Page " " Distiller
21 John H. Forsyth " " Cabinet maker
22 Henry Chrysler " " Blacksmith
23 David Pratt " " Shoe maker
24 John Goose of Raleigh Yeoman
25 William Harvey " "
26 William McIntosh " "
27 Daniel Crow " "
28 John Crow " "
29 Louis Dragon " "
30 Charles Lenover " "
31 Antoine Grandbois " "
32 Pierre Toulouse of Dover Yeoman
33 Charles Lauzon " "
34 Charles La Marche " "
35 Jean Petteau " "
36 Nicholas Ballard " " Blacksmith

Petty Jury List, undated 1830s, Praecepts, Essex County Court of General Quarter Sessions of the Peace Records, Archives of Ontario, RG 22-114.

Grand Jury

A grand jury of at least twelve and up to twenty-four men was called to serve at each session of court. Men who served on grand juries for the Assizes were usually magistrates or at least men of substance such as merchants and respectable farmers. Grand jurors for the Quarter Sessions were taken from the assessment rolls. They represented a large cross section of the population.[76]

The grand jurors met privately before each court session to determine whether or not the Crown had sufficient evidence to proceed to a criminal trial. They were provided with all of the prosecution's evidence and were permitted to interview prosecution witnesses (but not witnesses for the defence). In order to proceed, twelve of the grand jurors had to sign a bill of indictment, "true bill."[77]

The grand jury was also responsible for inspecting the district gaol and reporting on its condition, and recommending appropriate actions or legislation. Their report was called a "presentment." Grand jury presentments were sent to the magistrates at the Quarter Sessions or the judge presiding at the Assize as well as to the Provincial Secretary and Attorney General.[78]

> By 1839 one grand jury was so infuriated by the fact that "the presentments made for many years on this subject [horrific gaol conditions] have not been attended to by the Magistrates" that they sent their presentment directly to the Lieutenant-Governor with a covering letter, saying "nothing has been done" to improve a dreadful situation. The magistrates had claimed the responsibility lay with the sheriff, but the Niagara jurors, tired of lame excuses, wanted the Lieutenant-Governor

to remedy the problem. Their presentment characterized the gaol as "in a state not only disgraceful to the District but to a Civilized people."[79]

Grand juries (both of the Quarter Sessions and the Assizes) sometimes took it upon themselves to prepare presentments concerning other local concerns and sent them to magistrates and sometimes to the Lieutenant-Governor. These might entail asking for clemency for a convicted felon, calling attention to safety issues, or criticizing disruptive behaviour of local residents. For example, a grand jury presentment in the Niagara District in 1828 complained about "swine running loose within the city, people indiscriminately shooting muskets, and others driving horses, carriages, wagons, and carts recklessly and even more alarming, 'so many women of loose habits ... prowling our streets at all hours in the night.'"[80]

Petit or Trial Jury

A unique group of twelve jurors was chosen for each trial. The Act for the Regulation of Juries spelled out the procedure for choosing these juries. Shortly before the court was due to sit, the sheriff was to provide a list of eligible jurors, called a panel. The list had to contain the full names and addresses of at least thirty-two, and no more than forty-eight, residents of the district.[81] Members of the jury panel were summoned to appear in court on the first day of the session, where their names were written on separate slips of paper and put in a box. When the court began, an impartial officer of the court was to draw one name at a time until there were twelve jurors selected. Sometimes that required drawing more than twelve names, as some potential jurors might not have appeared in court (they would be fined), or might have their impartiality challenged by either the prosecution or defence.

The role of the petit jury was to evaluate the evidence presented to them and determine whether the accused had committed the offence for which he or she was charged. The verdict had to be unanimous.[82] The jury did not decide the sentence.

Upper Canadian juries were notoriously unpredictable. Even when the facts were beyond dispute, they sometimes refused to convict when they sympathized with the accused. The records don't usually give us any hints as to the reasoning of the jury, or the details of what went on during their deliberations, but unusual cases are sometimes reported in the newspaper. For example, at the Newcastle District Assizes in 1824, a man named William McIntosh was charged with violating customs by not reporting his vessel at port. Since the law was meant to discourage smuggling its breach was a serious offence. But the community was behind the defendant and believed that the charge was too harsh. The judge instructed the jury "to discard from their minds every thing like hardship on the part of the defendant; to consider merely the abstract question, whether a breach of the Revenue Law had been committed; and as this was admitted even by the defendant's counsel, to find for the Crown." After deliberating for half an hour, the jury acquitted McIntosh. Against precedent, the judge required the jury to explain their reasons for the verdict. When the foreman explained, the judge told the jury that their verdict was against the law and the evidence, and that they should change their verdict. The jury refused. Finally, the jury agreed to reconsider and went away for three hours. They came back with a handwritten, lengthy explanation of their original verdict. The judge started to lecture them again and the foreman replied, "he could not satisfy his conscience in no [sic] other manner than by the present verdict ... and that he would starve to death before he would alter his verdict." So the judge finally gave up and the verdict was recorded.[83]

Coroner's Jury

Coroner's juries were chosen by the local coroner from the sheriff's jury panels, in order to assist him in investigating deaths of a sudden, unexpected, or suspicious nature or that had occurred while the deceased was under the control of central authority (e.g., in police custody). The coroner's jury heard witness testimony, including the report of the coroner and any experts he called to give evidence.[84]

The coroner's jury was more like a grand jury than a petit jury in that it was charged with determining whether a crime had been committed, and if there was reasonable grounds to accuse a particular person with a crime. The coroner's jury was also expected to provide recommendations for further actions, regardless of any fault finding (such as safety procedures to prevent future accidents). The coroner's jury did not convict anyone. If they determined that a crime had been committed, the accused would be bound over for trial at the next sitting of the Assizes and tried before a petit jury, as with other capital crimes.[85]

While the records of the inquest itself have not survived, an 1834 petition written by members of a coroner's jury in Niagara provides an excellent example of the work of the jury.

> To the Worshipful, the Magistrates in Quarter Sessions assembled, the petition of sundry inhabitants living in the townships of Crowland, Wainfleet, Pelham and Thorald near the junction of the Welland Canal and feeder, humbly

sheweth, that a jury was called by Messrs David Thompson and Amos Bradshaw, two of his majesty's Justices of the Peace (who were under the necessity of acting in the absence of a coroner) to hold an inquest on the body of John McIntire on the 9th of March 1834 who was found dead in the Welland Canal on the evenening [*sic*] previous. That the jury upon examining the body of the deceased as far as circumstances would permit, were (from appearances) impressed with the idea that he had been violently bruised previous to his decease.

The jury considering it their duty, made such inquiry into the case as was in their power to make, and the result of their investigation was as follows. The deceased entered the house or Inn of Henry Sloan, Innkeeper at the Junction of the Canal and Feeder, in Crowland, on the evening of the 24th of Dec[r] 1833. That the deceased was sober when he entered the inn, but called for whiskey which he drank and became drunk, noisy, and quarrelsome. That there were several persons at the same inn, drinking and raffling. And that the deceased quarreled with several persons in the house — was at length put out of doors by the proprietor, Henry Sloan, that he was followed by a person who seemed angry: this person George Stuart and the deceased were found by H. Sloan, engaged out of doors, and parted by him when Stuart was put into the house, and the deceased left out, which appears to be the last that was seen of him until he was found on Saturday the 8th March 1834 in the Welland Canal dead.

The jury brought in a verdict "that the deceased John McIntire having been abused at the Inn of Henry Sloan, and turned out of the house, was supposed to have started for his own home but being in a state of intoxication, fell into the canal and was drowned."

That your petitioners, from the circumstances above related and from other evidence, are led to believe that Henry Sloan does not keep a peaceable, sober and quiet house — but on the contrary, that it is the resort of the Drunken and the dissolute. And they are well satisfied, that the above mentioned, awful, and lamentable catastrophe, was occasioned wholly by the deceased making an intemperate use of ardent spirits which were too plentifully furnished him, and being associated with the drunken and dissolute company that frequent that place.

That your petitioners humbley request, that your worships will compel the said Henry Sloan, to desist from selling spirituous liquors, and your petitioners as in duty bound will every pray.

Thorold, 18th March 1834

Signed: James Brown, Alexander Brown, William Davidson, Alcxr McReilly, John B McReilly, John Kellerns, Thomas Bald, Aaron Price, David P. Brown, Abraham Chapman, Peter Jennings, Peter Pettet, Andrew Moore, C.WW. Hellems, Enoch Shrigley and ?? ??[illegible].[86]

The Court of Quarter Sessions responded by issuing subpoenas to some of the petitioners, and one of the magistrates visited Henry Sloan. Sloan voluntarily closed his tavern and moved out of the district. [87]

The Legal Profession

In eighteenth-century England, courts didn't use lawyers. Trials were conducted by judges and juries who questioned witnesses, defendants, and accusers directly. In the 1750s, Crown officials began to organize prosecutions and defence lawyers began to challenge them.[88]

At first, treason was the only charge in which all defendants were entitled to legal counsel. An Act of 1836 guaranteed the right to professional legal counsel to all defendants in criminal cases.[89] However, as the general public associated lawyers with the elite who ran the government, few accused bothered to hire legal representation.[90]

In England there were two types of lawyers: barristers (also known as advocates), who specialized in litigating in court, and solicitors (also known as attorneys), who specialized in procedures, document drafting, and estate management. Solicitors also prepared cases for trial, but never went to court themselves.[91] Prospective barristers were called students-at-law and prospective attorneys were called articled clerks.[92] Barristers had more prestige than attorneys, but the attorney role was more lucrative as there was more work available (drawing up wills and property conveyances mostly).[93] Unlike in England, in Upper Canada one could practice as both a solicitor and barrister.[94]

In the first few years of the colony, lawyers were regulated by the legislature, which issued licences to practise.[95] However, that soon changed with the founding of the Law Society of Upper Canada in 1797. At that time, there were only thirty lawyers in the entire province. Only one was educated and trained as a barrister in London, England. One had been educated and trained in Montreal. The rest had no formal training or experience.[96]

The Law Society of Upper Canada was created as the organ of a self-governing profession empowered to set its own qualifications for admission.[97] In brief, the system was thus: the barristers voted for benchers, who formed "Convocation." They fixed the standard of education, conducted examinations, and called to the bar. Convocation also governed the education and examinations of solicitors.[98]

Legal Training

According to the 1797 Act that set up the Law Society of Upper Canada, each member of the Law Society could take one student-at-law. In 1803, the Act was modified to allow each member to take two (with the Attorney General and the Solicitor General being allowed three each). That was further modified in 1807 to allow each member to have four students.[99] At first, there were no criteria for law students. Each member could choose his own students however he wished. After five years of articling, most students were automatically called to the bar.[100] Generally, students-at-law were unpaid. In fact, some actually paid a fee for their "training," which generally consisted of doing all of the tedious "copying" work.[101] What legal education they received came mostly from private study and watching the operation of the court.[102]

Starting in 1819, admission to the law society (required before one could article) required the passing of entrance exam. This exam required applicants to translate an excerpt of Cicero from Latin to English (thus proving that they were well educated).[103] In 1825 the entrance exam was expanded, requiring applicants to demonstrate general knowledge of English, Grecian, and Roman history, acquaintance with one of the ancient Latin poets, acquaintance with celebrated prose works of the ancients, and a reasonable portion of mathematical instruction.[104] By the 1830s, entrance exams covered Latin and English composition, history, geography, and the elements of Euclid.[105]

In 1828, the Law Society introduced a new requirement: "term keeping." That meant that students had to attend the Court of King's Bench and board at Osgoode Hall while they were in town (the Court of King's Bench sat in the capital: York).[106] In the 1830s, the Law Society added the requirement that students living in or near the capital had to attend classes, lectures, and club meetings.[107]

The first final exam to test candidates before calling them to the bar was instituted in 1831.[108] These exams tested students' knowledge of the principles of law in England, the science of special pleading, the law of evidence, the law of trials at nisi prius, and the practice of courts.[109] In the first nine years that the test was administrated no one failed. Twenty-five to thirty new lawyers were called to the bar each year.[110] The failure rates increased sharply in the 1850s as the law society attempted to regulate the number of practicing lawyers.[111]

Up until 1850, fewer than 10 percent of the Law Society initiates had university degrees. In the 1850s that number peaked at 60 percent, then it dropped to about 30 percent for the rest of the nineteenth century.[112]

Despite its apparent informality, compared to the system we are currently familiar with, legal historian Blaine Baker tells us

OSGOODE HALL, ERECTED IN 1829–32.

Osgoode Hall, c. 1856, Toronto Reference Library, T33830.

that "the form of law training which evolved in Upper Canada between 1785 and 1889 was more intensive and more sophisticated than that which existed in England or most American jurisdictions at the time."[113]

The career of John Wilson is a fascinating example of the unique opportunities for practitioners of the law in Upper Canada. Wilson was the son of a poor Scottish weaver who had immigrated to Upper Canada around 1823, when Wilson was fourteen years old. The family settled on a farm in Lanark County. Three or four years later, Wilson contracted "a disease of the chest" and was advised to avoid heavy labour, so he moved into town and became a schoolteacher. In 1830, Wilson became a student-at-law in the office of James Boulton of Perth. While most law students were supported by their wealthy families, Wilson had to work in addition to his unpaid articling, tutoring Boulton's daughter and keeping the books of a local merchant in his spare time. One day in 1833, Wilson challenged another student-at-law to a duel, in defence of the honour and reputation of a young lady with whom he was friendly. His opponent

John Wilson, lawyer, judge, and legislator. Toronto Reference Library, T16864.

was considered a "crack shot" and was expected to win the duel
easily, but Wilson's shot was the fatal one. Wilson and his second immediately went to Perth and surrendered themselves to

the authorities. Two months later they were tried for murder in the Assize Court and acquitted, the judge having advised in his charge to the jury that "the practice of private combat has its immediate origin in high examples even of kings. Juries have not been known to convict when all was fair, yielding to the practices of society...." The following year, Wilson moved to London (Upper Canada), where he established a very successful law practice. He was also a strong proponent of education, frequently giving public lectures and donating his time to teach young boys the fundamentals of arithmetic and history. In 1842, he was appointed warden of the London District. In 1843, he acted as school superintendent, and in 1847 he ran for public office and was elected to the House of Assembly for London, serving until 1851 and again from 1854 to 1857. He briefly retired from public life, until his appointment as a judge in the Court of Common Pleas for Ontario from 1863 until his death in 1869.[114]

Personnel Records

Personnel records range from the very formal and spare, such as oaths of office and official commissions, to the personal papers of individual office holders. More senior personnel naturally left greater volumes of records. For more junior officers, accounts can be instructive, as they indicate the services the officer performed.

Note: This inventory only contains records that begin before 1841. Many other records will be available for the post-1841 period.

Officers of the Crown

Inventory

Attorney General and Solicitor General
- AO F44 John Beverley Robinson family fonds (he was Attorney General from 1812 to 1815, Solicitor General from 1815 to 1829, and Chief Justice from 1829 to 1862). Five bound diaries, scrapbook of commissions (and loose ones), papers relating to treason trial 1838, charges to the grand jury; mostly on microfilm.
- AO F4448 John White fonds. Diary 1792–1794 — on microfilm, MS 8350, published *Ontario History*, vol. XLVII, no. 4, 147–170.
- LSUC PF27 John Beverley Robinson fonds, 1812–1813. Fonds consists of a journal maintained by John Beverley Robinson while Acting Attorney General of Upper Canada during the War of 1812.

High Court Judges
- AO RG 22-390-1 Bench books of James B. Macaulay, 1827–1857.
- AO RG 22-390-2 Bench books of Sir John B. Robinson, 1829–1863.
- AO RG 22-390-3 Bench books of Christopher Hagerman, 1828–1829.
- AO RG 22-390-4 Bench books of Jonas Jones, 1837–1848.
- AO RG 22-545-0-2: Judges' Rolls: rolls of judges who swore an oath upon becoming barristers in the Court of Queen's Bench or in the Court of Common Pleas, 1829–1868.
- AO F44 John Beverley Robinson family fonds (he was

Attorney General from 1812 to 1815, Solicitor General from 1815 to 1829 and Chief Justice from 1829 to 1862). Five bound diaries, scrapbook of commissions (and loose ones), papers relating to treason trial 1838, charges to the grand jury; mostly on microfilm.

- AO F552 William Osgoode fonds. Letters describing his work as the first Chief Justice of Upper Canada, including a few court cases and judicial recordings.

- LAC RG5 B7 Civil secretary, applications for appointments to public offices Upper Canada and Canada West, 1803–1876.

- LSUC PF 8 William Osgoode collection, 1772–1824. Collection consists of correspondence received and sent by William Osgoode, first Chief Justice of Upper Canada. Two bound volumes entitled: "Osgoode Correspondence 1772–1823," and loose correspondence. The majority of the letters relate to Osgoode's personal life and only a few date from his time in Canada. The letters have been published in: *Friends of the Chief Justice: The Osgoode Correspondence in the Archives of the Law Society of Upper Canada*, Douglas Hay and Ruth Paley ed., The Law Society of Upper Canada, Toronto, 1990.

- LSUC PF20 James Buchanan Macaulay fonds, 1838. Fonds consists of a bench book maintained by Justice James Buchanan Macaulay during the trial for treason of suspects who were alleged to have participated in the December 1837 Duncombe Revolt.

Justices of the Peace
- AO RG 8-15 Magistrate Books, Volume 1, 1836–1842, MS 582 Reel 1, lists of appointments of magistrates by district and county.

- AO RG 8-23 Correspondence of the Provincial Secretary's Office for Canada West, 1832–1866, mostly pertaining to the appointment of Magistrates and Coroners, recommendations, complaints, petitions.

- AO RG 22-16 Johnstown District (Brockville) Court of General Quarter Sessions of Peace, Accounts, 1796–1845.

- AO RG 22-34 Newcastle District (Cobourg) Court of General Quarter Sessions of Peace, accounts, 1801–1848.

- AO RG 22-105 Western District (Windsor) Court of General Quarter Sessions of Peace, accounts, 1833–1842, MS 166.

- AO RG 22-111 Western District (Windsor) Court of General Quarter Sessions of Peace, accounts, 1818–1869, in Hiram Walker Collection, MS 205.

- LAC RG5 B7 Civil secretary, applications for appointments to public offices Upper Canada and Canada West, 1803–1876.

- LAC MG9 D8-14 Johnstown District collection: the papers of Edward Jessup, Clerk of the Peace 1800–1801, 102 pages. Series consists of papers preserved by Edward Jessup while Clerk of the Peace. Included are memorials of Edward Jessup and Sheriff Thomas Fraser for compensation for services, 1800–1801, eight pages; a letter from Jessup to the magistrates concerning the completion of the assessment rolls, 28 January 1801, two pages; and miscellaneous papers relating to prosecutions before the Court of General Quarter Sessions of the Peace for the Johnstown District. A list of individuals involved precedes the volumes, ninety-two pages.

- LAC R3800-0-3-E (formerly MG24 D108) Robert Nelles fonds 1782–1848. Series consists of chronologically arranged papers of Robert Nelles and his family, largely composed of correspondence that contains information about Nelles' business dealings in lumber and whisky, his family, and his political involvements. In addition to his family, Nelles corresponded with Joseph Brant, 1798–1803, Richard Beasley, 1800, and Thomas Scott, 1804. The reports and affidavits largely pertain to his career and activities as a member of Legislative Assembly and a Justice of the Peace, respectively. Nelles' family's active involvement in the 4th Regiment, Lincoln County Militia is recorded by the presence of a muster roll, 1814, and general orders, 1820, 1822.

- BULA Thompson, Frances Ann, *Local Authority and District Autonomy: The Niagara Magistracy and Constabulary, 1828–1841*, Ottawa: University of Ottawa, 1996. Unpublished thesis.

- NHS Records of Justice of the Peace, Francis Leigh Walsh (1824–1880).

- TUA United Counties of Northumberland and Durham. Court records fonds, 1803–1955: includes oaths of Coroners and Gaol Surgeons, commissions of Coroners and Magistrates, juror rolls and jury lists.

- TUA United Counties of Northumberland and Durham. Lists of office holders: jail surgeons, coroners, magistrates.

- *www.trentu.ca/admin/library/archives/84-020%20personnelucnd.htm*.

- TUA 71-006 John Huston fonds, 1818–1849. Includes his papers as Justice of the Peace.

- TUA 90-005 Victoria County fonds, 1834–1969: General Quarter Sessions of the Peace, includes jury records, accounts (majority are post-1860).

- UWO B155 London District Quarter Sessions Records, includes Accounts, 1831–1835.

- Armstrong, Frederick Henry, *Upper Canada Justices of the Peace and Association, 1788–1841*, Toronto: Ontario Genealogical Society, 2007. This is a list of all Justices of the Peace appointed during the Upper Canada period, with their dates of appointment and district.

Clerks of the Peace, Assize, and Crown

- AO RG 22-768: Correspondence of the Clerks of the Crown, 1825–1869, includes incoming letters and letterbooks.
- AO F526: Alexander McMartin fonds, 1796–1853: Records of McMartin's work as a Justice of the Peace include complaints, affidavits, writs, warrants, and recognisance. Records arising from his work as a bailiff include his appointment records, and writs of seizure. Records from his work as a Clerk of the Peace include receipts of land certificates, a writ ordering the sale of Roxborough land to pay property taxes, and an order for payment.
- LAC RG5 B7 Civil secretary, applications for appointments to public offices Upper Canada and Canada West, 1803–1876.
- LAC MG9 D8-14 Johnstown District collection: the papers of Edward Jessup, Clerk of the Peace 1800–1801, 102 pages. Series consists of papers preserved by Edward Jessup while Clerk of the Peace.
- NHS Thomas Welch Papers, Clerk of the Court, London District. Court papers, 1796–1816.

Coroners

- AO RG 8-23 Correspondence of the Provincial Secretary's Office for Canada West, 1832–1866 (mostly pertaining to the appointment of Magistrates and Coroners, recommendations, complaints, petitions).

- AO RG 22-16 Johnstown District (Brockville) Court of General Quarter Sessions of Peace, accounts, 1796–1845.
- AO RG 22-34 Newcastle District (Cobourg) Court of General Quarter Sessions of Peace, accounts, 1801–1848.
- AO RG 22-105 Western District (Windsor) Court of General Quarter Sessions of Peace, accounts, 1833–1842, MS 166.
- AO RG 22-111 Western District (Windsor) Court of General Quarter Sessions of Peace, accounts, 1818–1869 in Hiram Walker Collection, MS 205.
- AO RG 22-4986 Stormont, Dundas and Glengarry Counties, Court of General Quarter Sessions of Peace, coroner commissions, 1830–1914.
- AO RG 53-49 Registers of Coroners' Appointments, 1837–1874.
- TUA 90-005 Victoria County fonds, 1834–1969: General Quarter Sessions of the Peace, includes jury records, accounts (majority are post-1860).
- UWO B155 London District Quarter Sessions Records, includes accounts, 1831–1835.
- TUA United Counties of Northumberland and Durham. Court records fonds, 1803–1955: includes oaths of coroners and jail surgeons, commissions of coroners and magistrates, juror rolls and jury lists.
- TUA United Counties of Northumberland and Durham, Lists of office holders: jail surgeons, coroners, magistrates.
- *www.trentu.ca/admin/library/archives/84-020%20person-nelucnd.htm.*

Sheriffs

- AO RG 22-16 Johnstown District (Brockville) Court of General Quarter Sessions of Peace, accounts, 1796–1845.
- AO RG 22-34 Newcastle District (Cobourg) Court of General Quarter Sessions of Peace, accounts, 1801–1848.
- AO RG 22-105 Western District (Windsor) Court of General Quarter Sessions of Peace, accounts, 1833–1842, MS 166.
- AO RG 22-111 Western District (Windsor) Court of General Quarter Sessions of Peace, accounts, 1818–1869 in Hiram Walker Collection, MS 205.
- LAC RG5 B7 Civil secretary, applications for appointments to public offices Upper Canada and Canada West, 1803–1876.
- LAC MG9 D8-14 Johnstown District collection: the papers of Edward Jessup, Clerk of the Peace 1800–1801, 102 pages. Series consists of papers preserved by Edward Jessup while Clerk of the Peace. Included are memorials of Edward Jessup and sheriff Thomas Fraser for compensation for services, 1800–1801, eight pages; a letter from Jessup to the magistrates concerning the completion of the assessment rolls, 28 January 1801, two pages; and miscellaneous papers relating to prosecutions before the Court of General Quarter Sessions of the Peace for the Johnstown District. A list of individuals involved precedes the volumes, ninety-two pages.
- LAC R4029-0-2-E (formerly MG24 I8) MacDonell Family Fonds, Allan MacDonell papers, 1837–1868. Series consists of papers and records collected as sheriff of Gore, 1837–1843, relating primarily to the Rebellion of 1837.

- LAC R4024-0-6-E (formerly MG24 I26 volumes 44–48) Alexander Hamilton and family fonds, records of the sheriff and various courts of the Niagara District, 1818–1837.
- LAC R6180-0-5-E (formerly MG24 I27) John McEwan fonds, 1811–1868. Fonds consists of correspondence and papers of Captain John McEwan, including some legal documents acquired while he was sheriff of Essex County.
- LAC R3944-0-4-E (formerly MG24 I73) J. W. Dunbar Moodie fonds. Official correspondence received by Moodie while he was sheriff of the Victoria District, 1839–1863.
- LSUC PF18 William Hands fonds, 1819–1820. Fonds consists of a notebook maintained by William Hands while sheriff for the Western District, 1803–1833.
- TUA 90-005 Victoria County fonds, 1834–1969: General Quarter Sessions of the Peace, includes jury records, accounts (majority are post-1860).
- UWO B155 London District Quarter Sessions Records, includes accounts, 1831–1835.

Constables

- AO RG 22-16 Johnstown District (Brockville) Court of General Quarter Sessions of Peace, accounts, 1796–1845.
- AO RG 22-34 Newcastle District (Cobourg) Court of General Quarter Sessions of Peace, accounts, 1801–1848.
- AO RG 22-105 Western District (Windsor) Court of General Quarter Sessions of Peace, accounts, 1833–1842, MS 166.
- AO RG 22-111 Western District (Windsor) Court of General Quarter Sessions of Peace, accounts, 1818–1869, in Hiram Walker Collection, MS 205.

- BULA Thompson, Frances Ann, *Local Authority and District Autonomy: The Niagara Magistracy and Constabulary, 1828–1841*, Ottawa: University of Ottawa, 1996. Unpublished thesis.
- TCA Note: Toronto City Police records (fonds 38) start in 1849.
- TUA 90-005 Victoria County fonds, 1834–1969: General Quarter Sessions of the Peace, includes jury records, accounts (majority are post-1860).
- UWO B155 London District Quarter Sessions Records, includes accounts, 1831–1835.

Lawyers

There seem to be few records of the legal profession for the Upper Canada period.

The Law Society first began to keep and publish rolls of members, barristers, benchers, and treasurers in 1832.[114] However, no records were kept (or are known to survive) of entrance and bar exams, and there seem to be few early law office records. Those of which I am aware, are listed below.

Inventory

- AO RG 22-545-0-1: Attorneys' rolls (of oaths), rolls of barristers who swore an oath upon becoming barristers in the Court of Queen's Bench or in the Court of Common Pleas, 1802–1868.
- AO RG 22-761: Registers that were kept by the Crown Office, containing a list of attorneys and their agents. The information in these volumes includes: name of attorney,

residence, district, and agent. The registers are in chart form and are alphabetically arranged, 1834–1873.

- QUA Kirkpatrick-Nickle fonds, 1797–1938. The law firm was founded in Kingston by Thomas Kirkpatrick in 1828. The fonds consists of letterbooks, journals, ledgers, blotters, court dockets, and registry office books that reflect the business of the law firm in handling estates and cases.
- TPL S102 Larrat William Smith diaries, 1839–1905, 52 Volumes. Smith was a prominent Toronto lawyer. He began the diaries while articling with W.H. Draper. Most of the topics are personal, but some legal topics are mentioned.

Juries

Juror's panels are the lists of people eligible to serve on juries. These are prepared by the sheriff using the tax assessment rolls prepared by the Clerk of the Peace. Jurors' panels include the eligible jurors' names, their addresses (generally by lot and concession number, and township or village), and their occupations.

Jury lists are records of the actual jurors selected to serve at particular sessions of court. For Assize sessions they can be found among the praecepts records. These documents are directions from the judges of the Court of King's Bench to the sheriff of the district to summon jurors for the Assize.

Even if you're not interested in your ancestor's potential jury service, you might want to consider looking for these lists if the assessment rolls for his area are missing, as they will provide proof of his residence at the time.

Unfortunately, only a small number of these records survive for the pre-1841 period. In addition to the listings below, try checking any Clerk of the Peace or sheriffs' records labeled "filings," and "miscellaneous."

Inventory

- AO RG 22-142: Court of King's Bench praecepts series consists of the only three (1814, 1817, 1818) surviving Assize praecepts for the Home District. Attached to the praecepts are the sheriff's lists of grand and petit jurors summoned (panels).
- AO RG 22-372 Lincoln County (Niagara) Court of General Sessions of the Peace records, includes a letter, William Thorn to chairman, explaining his absence as a juror, 15 October 1833, film MS 10154.
- AO RG 22-1882 Essex County Minute books of the Boards of Selectors, 1839.
- AO RG 22-1886 Essex County Clerk of the Peace grand and petit jury lists, 1839.
- TPL L16 William Dummer Powell papers, B87: Papers regarding prisoners and trials throughout Upper Canada, 1794–1825. Mostly calendars of prisoners, also a few jury lists.
- TUA United Counties of Northumberland and Durham. Court records fonds, 1803–1955: includes juror rolls and jury lists.
- UWO B16 Jurors Book for the London District, 1836–1846.

CHAPTER SEVEN

What Changed After 1841?

The remainder of the nineteenth century saw several significant changes in the justice system. In general, the movement was toward greater professionalization, specialization, and standardization. Offices that began as part-time or temporary became full-time. Judicial and executive functions were gradually separated. Districts were abolished (except in the north) in favour of counties (in 1849) and their operation became more uniform.

Changes in Criminal Law

There were few major specific changes in the latter half of the nineteenth century. Mostly, they involved reducing the number of offences that were classed as "capital" (punishable by death).

The major changes occurred in 1859, when the Consolidated Statutes of Canada reduced capital offences to murder, treason, rape, poisoning or wounding with intent to murder, unlawfully abusing a girl under ten, buggery with man or beast, robbery with wounding, burglary with assault, arson, setting fire to or casting away a ship, or exhibiting a false signal endangering a ship.[1] In 1873 the options for sentencing for rape were expanded, so it was punishable by life in prison in addition to execution.[2]

Changes in Law Enforcement

A provincial statute of 1845 authorized the formation of a mounted police force of up to one hundred men to serve in districts where large-scale public works were in progress.[3] Gradually, municipal police forces grew during the nineteenth century. For example, in St. Catharines the first full-time officers were hired in 1845. By the time St. Catharines was incorporated as a city in 1876, it had a force of thirteen, consisting of a chief, two sergeants, and ten constables.[4] In Toronto, the first five full-time constables were hired in 1835. By 1855, the force was comprised of over fifty constables. A major reform took place in February 1859, when the constabulary was replaced with a new police force of fifty-one men and seven non-commissioned officers.[5]

The first salaried provincial constable was hired in 1875. He was joined by two additional detectives in 1897.[6]

Changes in Investigation

A major change took place in 1857, with the County Attorneys Act. This act provided for the appointment of a crown attorney for each county. The crown attorney took over the role of Clerk of the Peace and added the responsibility of preparing crown's case in local Assizes and supervising prosecutions at the Quarter Sessions. The change was intended to curb "malicious prosecutions" when people used the courts to settle private grudges.[7]

Changes in Adjudication

Before 1841 the Quarter Sessions were presided over by Justices of the Peace who might have no legal training. After 1841, the Quarter Sessions had to be chaired by district court judges who were required to be lawyers.[8] At the same time, mayors and aldermen acquired summary jurisdiction in Police Court, and could form a Mayor's Court with the addition of a jury.[9]

The Municipal Corporations Act of 1849 established Police or Magistrate's Courts in all towns with populations over 5,000. Cases were heard by police magistrates — police officers acting as Justices of the Peace to hear minor criminal cases. That helped speed up the process instead of waiting for the next Quarter Sessions. These courts had jurisdiction over same offences as the Quarter Sessions.[10]

Also in 1849, a Court of Appeal and Error was established for the province. It was renamed the Court of Appeal in 1881.

In Toronto, the Mayor's Court was replaced in 1851 by a Recorder's Court with a salaried police magistrate appointed to preside at Police Court. The magistrate didn't have to be a lawyer but the recorder did.[11]

In 1869, new legislation changed the name of the court to the Court of General Sessions of the Peace, changed the schedule to twice a year instead of quarterly, and required that it be presided over by county court judges (no longer by Justices of the Peace).[12]

At the same time, the legislation called the Speedy Trials Act established the County Judges' Criminal Courts, to allow trials by judge alone, where defendants waived the right to a trial before a jury. The jurisdiction of these courts was the same as the Quarter Sessions (i.e., all offences except murder, manslaughter, treason, piracy, rape, judicial corruption, libel, and frauds on the government). The intention was to help speed up the process, so people wouldn't have to wait for the next General Session.[13]

In 1875 a new level of court was established — the Supreme Court of Canada. In 1881 the Court of Queen's Bench merged with the Court of Common Pleas and the Court of Chancery to become the High Court of Justice of the Supreme Court of Ontario.[14]

One final change would come about near the close of the century. In 1892 the Criminal Code of Canada was created, limiting the number of offences that had to be handled by the High Court (then called the Court of Queen's Bench) to six: murder, manslaughter, treason, sedition, rape, and piracy. All other offences were moved to the three lower courts: Quarter Sessions, Police Magistrates Courts, and the County Judge's Criminal Courts.[15]

Changes in Sentencing

The stocks and pillory was abolished in 1841.[16]

Consolidated Statutes of Canada (1859) reduced capital offences to murder, treason, rape, poisoning or wounding with intent to murder, unlawfully abusing a girl under ten, buggery with man or beast, robbery with wounding, burglary with assault, arson, setting fire to or casting away a ship, or exhibiting a false signal endangering a ship.[17]

A new boys' reformatory was opened in 1859 at Penetanguishene as a special place for juvenile offenders.[18]

As of 1873, rape was no longer automatically a capital crime. It could instead be punished by life in prison.[19]

In 1874, a Central Prison was opened in Toronto to accommodate convicts sentenced to terms of hard labour too short to qualify them for the penitentiary (less than two years).[20]

In 1878, a reformatory for women and an attached "refuge" for girls were opened in Toronto. It was called the Ontario Industrial Refuge for Girls and Vanier Centre for Women (records begin in 1880).[21]

In 1887, the province's first industrial training school for boys was opened. In 1890, it was enacted that young offenders below the age of thirteen should be sent to these instead of Penetanguishene. In the 1890s, industrial schools for girls began to be set up.[22]

Changes in Personnel

Starting in 1845, district judges had to have five years practice at the bar before they could be appointed, and they were no longer permitted to practise privately while serving as a judge.[23]

In 1850, legislation changed the way jury panels were selected. Instead of being prepared by the sheriff they were put under the control of a committee of elected municipal officials called "boards of selectors."[24]

Other Changes

Starting in 1841 other options for the housing and protection of disabled people became available. A temporary "lunatic asylum" was opened in Toronto in 1841. A permanent replacement for it, called the Provincial Lunatic Asylum, was completed in 1851.[25] The first institution for the deaf and dumb opened in 1870 in Belleville.

CHAPTER EIGHT

Research Advice and Records by District

As most records are arranged by district, it's helpful to have a district map for the period that you are interested in.

You will also need to know the reigns of monarchs and the names for the old court terms (see the Appendix).

You may need to search a variety of records to get the "full picture," as people didn't neatly confine their activities to one jurisdiction, or their appearances to one court. One notorious character, Daniel Sullivan, appeared in at least three courts over his violent "career." Starting in May 1832, he appeared before the Home District Quarter Sessions at least five times, variously charged with assault and battery, riot, and affray.[1] Between 1834 and 1836 Sullivan was charged with assault seven times in the Toronto Mayor's Court.[2] His appearance on 1 September 1834 was for beating up an Orangeman who had joined a meagre Orange parade.

Eventually, he graduated to the Assize Court, where he was convicted of assault with intent to murder in November 1837, and sentenced to Kingston Penitentiary for three years.[3]

He seems to have kept relatively calm for a while after his

release in March 1839 (he was released early for good behaviour).[4] However, in 1848 he was back before the Quarter Sessions, on trial for riot after he, his brother Patrick, and a third man attacked fourteen armed Orangemen in a tavern.

Newspaper accounts help fill in the context, revealing that the Roman Catholic Sullivan's adversaries were nearly all Orangemen or high Tories and the disputes were politically motivated, occurring during elections and Orange demonstrations. The Orange newspaper, the *Toronto Recorder*, reported "not a row of any consequence takes place but the name of Sullivan is connected with it," and "this name carries terror along with it, to every peaceable and well-minded citizen."[5]

These activities are revealed in the records of three different courts, two sets of penitentiary records, one private fonds (the Assize judge's bench book), and five newspapers — which are preserved in three distinct archives!

• • •

Finally, it's important not to overlook civil records. For many reasons, including because people didn't see them as separate, and because the same officials at the same time dealt with cases at Quarter Sessions and Assizes, criminal and civil courts often dealt with same or similar cases, or different aspects of the same case, as the example of the convoluted dispute between the residents of Burford in 1839 reveals (see Chapter Five: Public Opinion).

District Maps

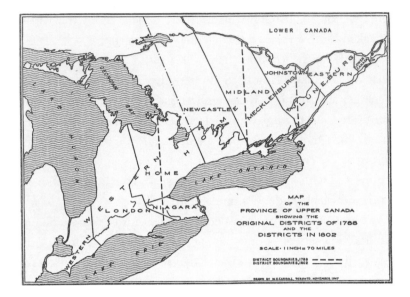

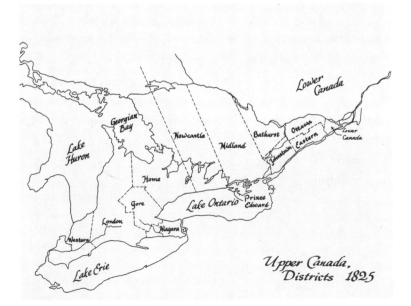

Opposite page, above:"The Districts of Upper Canada, 1788-1849" by George Spragge, Ontario Historical Society Papers and Records, Volume 59, (1967).

Opposite page, below: Map of Upper Canada in 1825 drawn by William Fraser for Genealogy in Ontario: Searching the Records by Brenda Dougall Merriman published by the Ontario Genealogical Society. Used with permission.

This Page: Map of Canada West in 1845 drawn by William Fraser for Genealogy in Ontario: Searching the Records by Brenda Dougall Merriman published by the Ontario Genealogical Society. Used with permission.

R. vs. Sullivan, Home District Assizes March-April 1837, Bench book of John Beverly Robinson, Archives of Ontario, RG 22-390-2 Box 23.

Records by District

Note: This inventory only contains records that begin before 1841. Many other records will be available for the post-1841 period. These listings are abbreviated. For full descriptions, see listings in chapter records sections.

Province-Wide, or No Specific District

- AO RG 4-1, Boxes 6-7 Crown Prosecutions Case files, 1799–1843.
- AO RG 8-15 Magistrate Books, Volume 1, 1836–1842, MS 582 Reel 1.
- AO RG 8-23 Correspondence of the Provincial Secretary's Office for Canada West, 1832–1866.
- AO RG 22-125 Court of King's Bench Term Books, 1794–1843.
- AO RG 22-134 Central Criminal Assize minute books, 1792–1848.
- AO RG 22-135 Court of King's/Queen's Bench Criminal Assize rough minute books, 1792–1849.
- AO RG 22-138 Court of King's Bench Criminal Assize Filings, 1792–1799, 1815–1819.
- AO RG 22-142: Court of King's Bench praecepts.
- AO RG 22-143 Court of King's Bench records of high treason trials of 1814, 1814–1824.
- AO RG 22-144 Alien Act Commissions, inquisitions and related records, 1815–1830.
- AO RG 22-145 Court of King's Bench record of high treason trials of 1838.
- AO RG 22-390-1 Bench books of James B. Macaulay, 1827–1857.
- AO RG 22-390-2 Bench books of Sir John B. Robinson, 1829–1863.
- AO RG 22-390-3 Bench books of Christopher Hagerman, 1828–1829.

- AO RG 22-390-4 Bench books of Jonas Jones, 1837–1848.
- AO RG 22-545-0-1: Attorneys' Rolls (of oaths), 1802–1868.
- AO RG 22-545-0-2: Judges' Rolls, 1829–1868.
- AO RG 22-761: Registers of attorneys and their agents, 1834–1873.
- AO RG 22-766: Estreats and Miscellaneous Register, 1807–1817.
- AO RG 22-768: Correspondence of the Clerks of the Crown, 1825–1869.
- AO RG 53-49 Registers of Coroners' Appointments, 1837–1874.
- AO F31 Jarvis-Powell Papers.
- AO F44 John Beverley Robinson family fonds.
- AO F552 William Osgoode fonds.
- AO F4448 John White fonds.
- LSUC PF20 James Buchanan Macaulay fonds, 1838.
- LSUC PF27 John Beverley Robinson fonds, 1812–1813.
- LAC RG5 A1 Civil secretary, Correspondence (incoming) also known as the Upper Canada Sundries.
- LAC RG5 A2 Civil secretary, Correspondence (outgoing), drafts of replies.
- LAC RG7 G16 Civil secretary, Correspondence (outgoing), replies sent.
- LAC RG5 B7 Civil secretary, applications for appointments to public offices Upper Canada and Canada West, 1803–1876.
- LAC RG5 B27 Upper Canada and Canada West: Civil and Provincial Secretaries. Include Gaol calendars and prison returns by district, 1823–1847.
- LAC RG5 B29 Clerks of the Peace, Extracts of Fines, 1811–1833.

- LAC RG5 B36, B37 Civil Secretary, records relating to Rebellions. Upper Canada. Minutes of proceedings for the trials conducted by the magistrates, 1837–1838.
- LAC RG5 B39 Civil Secretary, records relating to Rebellions. Upper Canada. Records of the inquiry into the conduct of Colonel John Prince at the Battle of Windsor, 1839.
- LAC RG5 B40, B41 Civil Secretary, records relating to Rebellions. Upper Canada. Proceedings of the courts martial at Fort Henry, Kingston, 1838–1839.
- LAC RG5 B43 Civil Secretary, records relating to Rebellions. Upper Canada. Documents relating to the prosecution of Alexander McLeod for the destruction of the Caroline, 1841.
- LAC RG5 B44 Civil Secretary, records relating to Rebellions. Upper Canada. Claims for losses incurred during the Rebellions, 1846–1847.
- LAC RG 13 D1 Operational Records of the Penitentiary Branch, 1834–1962.
- LAC R188-36-2-E (formerly RG13-F-1) Dept of Justice fonds, Office of the Attorney General of Canada West, 1800–1866.
- LAC RG 68 Registrar General: Warrants and Pardons, 1818–1953.
- LAC RG 73 Kingston Penitentiary Registers, 1835–1974, T1943-T2029.
- "Hugh Armstrong's List of Convict Deaths at Kingston Penitentiary, 1835–1915." *www.cangenealogy.com/armstrong/kpart.htm.*
- BULA Upper Canada: Schedule of accounts prepared for the Commons House of Assembly, in pursuance of an address of that House to His Excellency Sir Peregrine

Maitland, K.C.B., Lieutenant-Governor, &c. &c. &c. 1816–1821.

- LSUC PF 8 William Osgoode collection, 1772–1824.
- TPL L16 William Dummer Powell papers.
- Armstrong, Frederick Henry. *Upper Canada Justices of the Peace and Association, 1788–1841.* Toronto: Ontario Genealogical Society, 2007.
- Corupe, Linda. *Upper Canadian Justice (Early Assize Court Records of Ontario), Volume 1 (1792–1809).* Bolton, ON: Linda Corupe, 2004. Complete transcriptions of the cases of the Court of Oyer and Terminer and General Gaol Delivery for the entire Province of Upper Canada, including verdicts, jury lists, and sureties; they also contains extensive appendices and end notes.
- Corupe, Linda. *Upper Canadian Justice (Early Assize Court Records of Ontario),*
- *Volume 2 (1810–1818).* Bolton, ON: Linda Corupe, 2008. This volume contains several historically important and renowned trials from the period, such as the Ancaster "Bloody Assize" of 1814 (the trials of those accused of treason during the War of 1812–1814).
- Harrison, Robert A. *A Digest of Reports of all Cases Determined in the Queen's Bench and Practice Courts for Upper Canada From 1823 to 1851 Inclusive [microform]: Being From the Commencement of Taylor's Reports to the End of Vol. VII Upper Canada Reports, [Cameron's Digests Included]: With an Appendix Containing the Digests of Cases Reported in Vol. VIII Upper Canada Reports 1852.* H. Rowsell (Canadian Institute of Historical Microreproductions (CIHM), fiche 10817).

Bathurst District

- AO RG 22-75 Lanark County (Perth) Court of General Quarter Sessions of Peace minutes, 1823–1896.
- AO RG 22-2843 Lanark County (Perth) Jail Records, 1837–1863. TPL Assizes of Upper Canada. Minutes by the Clerk of the Assize, R. Hervey Jr., Bathurst District, 19–23 September 1837.
- LAC R4419-0-0-E (formerly MG24 I57) 1833–34, Robert Lyon collection.

Brock District

- No known district-level records.

Colborne District

- PCMA Peterborough County Court fonds, 1830–1909.
- TUA 71-006 John Huston fonds, 1818–1849.

Dalhousie District

No known district-level records.

Eastern District

- AO RG 22-65 Ottawa District (L'Original) Court of General Quarter Sessions of Peace minutes, 1816–1869.

- AO RG 22-4986 Stormont, Dundas, and Glengarry United Counties, Court of General Quarter Sessions of Peace, coroner commissions, 1830–1914.
- AO F526: Alexander McMartin fonds, 1796–1853.
- LAC MG9 D8-8 Records Relating to the Eastern District: Record Book of the Court of General Quarter Session of Peace, 1826–1849.
- LAC MG9 D8-21 Court of General Quarter Sessions of the Peace, Luneburg District 1789–1827, Proceedings (photocopy).
- LSUC PF16-1 Luneburg District [Eastern] — Court of General Quarter Sessions of the Peace minute book, 1789–1802.
- QUA Upper Canada. Court of Quarter Sessions fonds. Lunenburg Quarter Session, 1789–1802. Microfilm copy of originals in Law Society of Upper Canada.
- TPL L16 William Dummer Powell papers.

Gore District

- AO RG 20-72 Gore District/Wentworth County (Hamilton) Jail Records, 1832–1975.
- LAC R4029-0-2-E (formerly MG24 I8) MacDonell Family Fonds, Allan MacDonell papers, 1837–1868.
- MUML Marjorie Freeman Campbell Collection, Typescript of Hamilton Police Village Minutes, 1833–1850.
- "Index to Gore District Debtors and Creditors, 1832–1849," *www.uppercanadagenealogy.com.*

Home (Nassau) District

- AO RG 20-100 Home District/York County (Toronto) Jail Records, 1837–1975.
- AO RG 22-94 York County (Toronto) Court of General Quarter Sessions of Peace minutes, 1800–1957, MS 251.
- AO RG 22-95 Home District (Toronto) Court of General Quarter Sessions of Peace rough minutes, 1836–1917.
- AO RG 22-96 York County (Toronto) Court of General Quarter Sessions of Peace filings, 1796–1799, 1828, 1832, 1838.
- AO RG 22-97 Home District (York/Toronto) Court of General Quarter Sessions of Peace, estreats, 1800–1845.
- TPL S102 Larrat William Smith diaries, 1839–1905.
- TPL S113 Alexander Wood papers, 1798–1837.
- TPL S125 Samuel Peters Jarvis papers, B68 Papers regarding the Jarvis/Ridout duel, 1815–1828.
- TPL General Quarter Sessions of the Peace for the Home District, Minutes, 13 March 1800–17 October 1801.
- TPL General Quarter Sessions of the Peace for the Home District, Minutes, 10 April 1801–7 February 1867. Typescript.
- TPL S278 Toronto Jail Statistical Registers, 1838–1877.
- TPL L16 William Dummer Powell papers. Unbound legal papers and notebooks: includes rough minutes for Assize sessions, including Home District, 16 October 1820.
- TCA fonds 95 (formerly RG7 Series E) Toronto Mayor's Court fonds.
- TCA fonds 200 series 255 Former City of Toronto by-laws, 1834–1997.

- TCA fonds 200 Series 362 (formerly RG7 Series B) Mayor's Office Letterbook, November 1834 to July 1844.
- TCA fonds 200 series 1077 Toronto Council minutes, 1836–1884.
- TCA fonds 200 series 1081 Toronto Council papers, 1834–1896.
- TCA Note: Toronto City Police records (fonds 38) start in 1849.
- "Minutes of the Court of General Quarter Sessions of the Peace for the Home District, 13th March, 1800 to 28th December, 1811." In *Twenty-First Report of the Department of Public Records and Archives of Ontario,* edited by Alexander Fraser, 1932.

Huron District

- AO GS microfilm, Huron County, Court of General Quarter Sessions of Peace, coroner's records, 1841–1904.
- HCM File of notes from the Committee that oversaw the building of the Gaol, 1839–1841.

Johnstown District

- AO RG 22-12 Leeds and Grenville United Counties (Brockville), Court of General Quarter Sessions of Peace minutes, 1800–1956.
- AO RG 22-14 Johnstown District (Brockville), Court of General Quarter Sessions of Peace, Case Files, 1802–1846.
- AO RG 22-16 Johnstown District (Brockville) Court of General Quarter Sessions of Peace, Accounts.

- AO RG 22-19 Johnstown District (Brockville) Court of General Quarter Sessions of the Peace Estreats, 1803–1837.
- LAC MG 9 D8-14 Johnstown District collection
- QUA Prescott Police Board Minute books, 1834–1850. Microfilmed copy.
- TPL L16 William Dummer Powell papers. Unbound legal papers and notebooks: includes rough minutes for Assize sessions, Johnston District, August 1825.

London District

- AO RG 22-63 London District (London) Court of General Quarter Sessions of the Peace Estreats, 1821–1831.
- AO RG 22-3395 Middlesex County/London District, Court of General Quarter Sessions of Peace, coroner's records, 1841–1893.
- AO GS microfilm Middlesex County/London District, Court of General Quarter Sessions of Peace, coroner's records, 1831–1835.
- LAC MG 9 D8-20 London District papers, Court of General Quarter Sessions of the Peace, London District 1800–1809, Procedings (photocopy).
- TPL General Quarter Sessions of the Peace for the London District, Minutes, 1800–1809, printed.
- TPL Assizes of Upper Canada. Minutes by the Clerk of the Assize, R. Hervey Jr., London District, 23–25 May 1837.
- TPL L16 William Dummer Powell papers, Unbound legal papers and notebooks: includes rough minutes for Assize sessions at London District, August 1818.

- UWO B16 Jurors Book for the London District, 1836–1846.
- UWO B155 London District Quarter Sessions Records.
- UWO B636 Minutes of the Court of Quarter Sessions, London District, 1813–1820, Volume 62.
- UWO E44 Correspondence and accounts relative to the London District courthouse and gaol, 1826–1828.
- UWO M779–M780 London District Court of Quarter Sessions, minutes, 1814–1853, microfilm.
- UWO M1247 London District Court of Quarter Sessions, minutebook, 1800–1809, microfilm.
- UWO JS1721.O7L78.3.A85 Court of Quarter Sessions of the Peace, schedule or table of fees.
- NHS Thomas Welch Papers, Clerk of the Court, London District. Court Papers, 1796–1816.
- "Minutes of the Court of General Quarter Sessions of the Peace for the London District, 1 April, 1800 to 12 September, 1809 and 4 December, 1813 to 26 December, 1818." In *Twenty-Second Report of the Department of Public Records and Archives of Ontario*, Alexander Fraser ed., 1933.

Midland (Mecklenburg) District

- AO RG 22-54 Midland District (Kingston) Court of General Quarter Sessions of Peace minutes, 1800–1849.
- LSUC PF16-2 Mecklenburg District [Midland] — Court of General Quarter Sessions of the Peace minute books, 1789–1827.
- QUA Upper Canada. Court of Quarter Sessions fonds. Mecklenburg Quarter Session, 1790–1816. Microfilm copy.
- QUA Kirkpatrick-Nickle fonds, 1797–1938.

- TPL Assizes of Upper Canada. Minutes by the Clerk of the Assize, R. Hervey Jr., Midland District, 3–14 October 1837.
- TPL L16 William Dummer Powell papers, unbound legal papers and notebooks: includes rough minutes for Assize sessions, including Midland District, August–September 1820 and August 1825.
- Corupe, Linda. *Minutes of the Court of Quarter Sessions of the Peace, Mecklenburg/Midland District. Volume 1: 1789–1816.* Bolton, ON: Linda Corupe, [c2001].
- Corupe, Linda. *Minutes of the Court of Quarter Sessions of the Peace, Midland District, Volume 2: 1832–1840.* Bolton, ON: Linda Corupe, 2001.
- Corupe, Linda. *Minutes of the Court of Quarter Sessions of the Peace, Midland District, Volume 3: 1841–1849.* Bolton, ON: Linda Corupe, 2002.

Newcastle District

- AO RG 20-66 Administrative Records of the Cobourg Jail, 1834–1975, MS 2720.
- AO RG 22-29 Newcastle District (Cobourg) Court of General Quarter Sessions of Peace minutes, 1802–1893, MS 698, Reels 1-2.
- AO RG 22-31 Newcastle District (Cobourg) Court of General Quarter Sessions of Peace case files, 1802–1846.
- AO RG 22-32 Newcastle District (Cobourg) Court of General Quarter Sessions of the Peace filings, 1803–1848.
- AO RG 22-34 Newcastle District Court of General Quarter Sessions of the Peace accounts, 1801–1848.
- AO RG 22-38 Newcastle District (Cobourg) Court of

General Quarter Sessions of Peace, grand jury present-
ments, 1822–1841.

- AO RG 22-41 Newcastle District (Cobourg) Court of
General Quarter Sessions of the Peace Estreats, 1837–
1847.
- AO RG 22-43 Newcastle District (Cobourg) Jail
Records, 1820–1846.
- AO RG 22-3788 Newcastle District, Court of General
Quarter Sessions of Peace, coroner's records, 1821–1848.
- PCMA Peterborough County Court fonds, 1830–1909.
- TUA 90-005 Victoria County fonds, 1834–1969.
- TUA United Counties of Northumberland and Durham.
Court records fonds, 1803–1955.
- TUA United Counties of Northumberland and Durham,
lists of office holders: jail surgeons, coroners, magistrates
*www.trentu.ca/admin/library/archives/84-020%20person-
nelucnd.htm.*
- TUA United Counties of Northumberland and Durham,
Index to Coroner's Inquests: *www.trentu.ca/admin/library/
archives/84-020%20inquestucnd.htm.*
- TPL L16 William Dummer Powell papers, unbound legal
papers and notebooks, includes rough minutes for Assize
sessions, including Newcastle District, Michaelmas Term
1819.
- "Index of Cobourg Jail Inmates, 1832–1848," *www.ontar-
iogenealogy.com/cobourgcriminal.html.*

Niagara District

- AO RG 22-372 Lincoln County Court of General
Quarter Sessions of Peace records, 1828–1919.

- AO RG 22-3195 Lincoln County Court of General Quarter Sessions of Peace, coroner's records, 1834–1917.
- LAC R3800-0-3-E (old MG24 D108) Robert Nelles fonds 1782–1848.
- LAC RG5 B38 Civil Secretary, records relating to Rebellions. Upper Canada. Contemporary copies of the 1839 proceedings in the Court of Queen's Bench in England resulting in the release of ten out of twenty-three men from the Niagara District intended for transportation to Australia.
- LAC R4024-0-6-E (formerly MG24 I26 volumes 44–48) Alexander Hamilton and family fonds, Records of the sheriff and various courts of the Niagara District, 1818–1837.
- BULA McEwen, Ann Alexandra. Crime in the Niagara district, 1827–1850. Guelph: University of Guelph, Dept. of History, 1991. Unpublished Thesis.
- BULA Thompson, Frances Ann. *Local Authority and District Autonomy: The Niagara Magistracy and Constabulary, 1828–1841.* Ottawa: University of Ottawa, 1996. Unpublished thesis.

Ottawa District

- No known district-level records.

Prince Edward District

- AO RG 22-83 Prince Edward County (Picton), Court of General Quarter Sessions of Peace minutes, 1834–1908.

- TPL Assizes of Upper Canada. Minutes by the Clerk of the Assize, R. Hervey Jr., Prince Edward District, 27–30 September 1837.

Simcoe District

- No known district-level records.

Talbot District

- NHS Records of Justice of the Peace, Francis Leigh Walsh (1824–1880).

Victoria District

- AO RG 22-09 Hastings County (Belleville) Court of General Quarter Sessions of Peace, minutes, 1837–1866.
- LAC R3944-0-4-E (formerly MG24 I73) J. W. Dunbar Moodie fonds. Official correspondance received by Moodie while he was sheriff of the Victoria District 1839–1863.
- TUA 90-005 Victoria County fonds, 1834–1969.

Wellington District

- AO RG 40-70 Wellington County (Guelph) Jail Records, 1840–1977.

Western (Hesse) District

- AO RG 22-103 Essex County (Windsor) Court of General Quarter Sessions of Peace minutes, 1821–1886.
- AO RG 22-105 Western District (Windsor) Court of General Quarter Sessions of Peace, accounts, 1833–1842.
- AO RG 22-106 Western District (Windsor) Court of General Quarter Sessions of Peace, grand jury present-ments, 1794–1874.
- AO RG 22-107 Western District (Windsor) Court of General Quarter Sessions of Peace, rough minutes, 1835–1859 in Hiram Walker Collection.
- AO RG 22-108 Western District (Windsor) Court of General Quarter Sessions of Peace, minutes of the chair-man, 1836–1845 in Hiram Walker Collection.
- AO RG 22-109 Western District (Windsor) Court of General Quarter Sessions of Peace, case files, 1821–1859 in Hiram Walker Collection.
- AO RG 22-110 Western District (Windsor) Court of General Quarter Sessions of Peace, filings, 1822–1859 in Hiram Walker Collection.
- AO RG 22-111 Western District (Windsor) Court of General Quarter Sessions of Peace, accounts, 1818–1869 in Hiram Walker Collection.
- AO RG 22-112 Western District (Windsor) Court of General Quarter Sessions of Peace, convictions by Justices of the Peace 1835–1864 in Hiram Walker Collection.
- AO RG 22-116 Western District (Windsor) Court of General Quarter Sessions of Peace, grand jury present-ments, 1833–1859 in Hiram Walker Collection.
- AO RG 22-118 Western District (Windsor) Court of General Quarter Sessions of Peace, lists of constables,

1838–1857 in Hiram Walker Collection.

- AO RG 22-119 Western District (Windsor) Court of General Quarter Sessions of Peace, correspondence, 1792–1881 in Hiram Walker Collection.
- AO RG 22-120 Western District (Windsor) Court of General Quarter Sessions of Peace, miscellaneous, 1808–1853 in Hiram Walker Collection.
- AO RG 22-1826 Western District Court of General Quarter Sessions of Peace, coroner's records, 1835–1836.
- AO RG 22-1882 Essex County Minute books of the Boards of Selectors, 1839.
- AO RG 22-1886 Essex County Clerk of the Peace grand and petit jury lists, 1839.
- AO RG 22-1894 Western District (Sandwich) Jail Records.
- LAC R6180-0-5-E (formerly MG24 I27) John McEwan fonds, 1811–1868.
- LAC MG9 D8-33 Proceedings of the Court of General Quarter Sessions of the Peace, Western District 1799–1802.
- LSUC PF18 William Hands fonds, 1819–1820. Fonds consists of a notebook maintained by William Hands while sheriff for the Western District (1803–1833).

APPENDIX

Reigns of Monarchs

George III, 1760–1820
George IV, 1820–1830
William IV, 1830–1837
Victoria 1837–1901

Court Terms

Hilary: January to April
Easter: April to May
Trinity. June to July
Michaelmas: October to December

Currency and Relative Worth

£ pound = 20 shillings

s. shilling = 12 pence

d. penny

Comparing nineteenth-century values with today's values is extremely difficult. Economists describe at least a dozen different methods, which result in extremely different results. A good source for detailed description of these methods, along with automatic calculators, is the Economic History Services "How Much is That?" website: *http://eh.net/hmit*, and the Measuring Worth website: *www.measuringworth.com/index.html*.

The measure that I find most helpful is to compare typical skilled labourer's wages then and now to give a rough idea of relative worth. According to "Colonization Circular Issued by Her Majesty's Colonial Land and Emigration Commissioners, 13 May 1843," skilled labourers, such as bakers, blacksmiths, plumbers, masons, and millwrights could expect daily wages from 5 to 9s. By comparison, Statistics Canada tells us that in January 2010, the average hourly wage for people working in the trades is $22.34, *www40.statcan.ca/l01/cst01/labr69a-eng.htm*.

Thus, using wages as a basis of measurement, 7s. in 1843 (inflation averaged less than 1 percent annually during the Upper Canada period, so this figure should hold fairly well for the period) was roughly equivalent to $180 now, so £1 was about $514.

By this measure, the average fine for assault and battery was about $128. The heaviest fine a person could receive at the Quarter Sessions was $2,570 and the Chief Justice (the highest judicial office in Upper Canada) earned about $500,000 per year.

In *The Time Traveller's Guide* by Althea Douglas (Toronto: Dundurn Press, 2010), you can find further and detailed discussion of what certain sums of money could purchase during the Upper Canada period.

GLOSSARY

Affray: A fight between two or more persons in a public place.

Assize Court: Colloquial name for the Court of Oyer and Terminer and General Gaol Delivery, a commission of the High Court of Upper Canada.

Bailiff: A civil officer entrusted with the duties of inspecting chimneys and buildings for fire safety, monitoring the use of weights and measures in markets, controlling domestic animals, and so on. Often used interchangeably with the term "constable" in early records.

Board of Police: Elected town government, headed by a mayor. Within the town limits, the board of police had special jurisdiction to decide minor cases without a jury.

Burglary: Breaking and entering a home with intent to commit a crime, or committing a crime and then breaking out of a home. Originally, burglary only applied to nighttime activities.

Estreat: An extraction from the records of a court, often pertaining to fines or recognizances that were forfeited

Ignoramus: Endorsement that the foreman of a jury placed on the indictment of a criminal charge when the jury wished to "ignore" the charge. The same as "no bill."

Larceny: Legal term for theft — taking away the personal property of someone else without their permission, with the intent of making it your own.

Magistrate: The colloquial term for Justice of the Peace.

Mayor's Court: A court with the same powers as the Courts of Quarter Sessions, but operating within a city.

Nolle Prosequé: The Latin expression for "unwilling to prosecute."

Police Court: A summary court (without a jury) operating within a town with "police" powers.

Police Village: A village that has been given "police" powers, meaning limited self-government (generally to pass by-laws pertaining to health and safety).

Puisne: From the French "puis ne," meaning later born, or junior in rank. Pronounced "puny."

Quarter Sessions: The short form for the Court of General Quarter Sessions of the Peace — the lower court in Upper Canada.

Recognizance: An obligation of record, entered into before some court or magistrate, whereby the party bound acknowledges (recognizes) that he or she owes a debt to the government or Crown, subject to a condition that the obligation to pay shall be avoided if he shall do some particular act, such as keeping the peace or appearing in court.

Robbery: Larceny by threat of violence.

Writ of Certiorari: To have a case removed to a higher court.

READING LIST / BIBLIOGRAPHY

Angle, Terry. "Prisoners of the Bicentennial Era: A Peek at Their Heritage." *Correctional Options* 4 (1984), 14–17.

Armstrong, Frederick Henry. "The York Riots of March 23, 1832." *Ontario History* 55 (1963), 61–72.

Armstrong, Frederick H. *Handbook of Upper Canadian Chronology.* Revised edition. Toronto: Dundurn Press, 1985.

Atkinson, Logan. "The Impact of Cholera on the Design and Implementation of Toronto's First Municipal By-Laws, 1834." *Urban History Review/Revue d'histoire urbaine* 30, No. 2 (March 2002), 3–15.

Backhouse, Constance. *Petticoats and Prejudice: Women and the Law in Nineteenth Century Canada.* Toronto: Women's Press, 1991.

Baechre, Rainer. "Trying the Rebels: Emergency Legislation and the Colonial Executive's Overall Legal Strategy in the Upper Canadian Rebellion." *Canadian State Trials*, Volume 2. Murray Greenwood and Barry Wright eds. Toronto: Law Society of Upper Canada and University of Toronto Press, 2002.

Baechre, Rainer. "Origins of the Penitentiary System in Upper Canada." *Ontario History* 79 No. 3 (1977), 185–207.

Baker, G. Blaine. "Legal Education in Upper Canada 1785–1889: The Law Society as Educator." *Essays in the History of Canadian Law*, Volume II, David H. Flaherty ed. Toronto: University of Toronto

Press for the Osgoode Society, 1983.

Baker, G. Blaine. "'So Elegant a Web': Providential Order and the Rule of Secular Law in Early Nineteenth-Century Upper Canada." *University of Toronto Law Journal*, 38 No. 2 (1988), 184–205.

Banks, Margaret A. "The Evolution of the Ontario Courts 1788–1981." *Essays in the History of Canadian Law*, Volume II, David H. Flaherty ed. Toronto: University of Toronto Press for the Osgoode Society, 1983.

Beattie, J.M. *Attitudes toward Crime and Punishment in Upper Canada 1830–1850: A Documentary Study.* Toronto: Working Paper of the Centre of Criminology, University of Toronto, 1977.

Bellomo, J. Jerald. "Upper Canadian Attitudes Towards Crime and Punishment (1832–1851)." *Ontario History* 64 No. 2 (1972), 11–26.

Betts, George. "Municipal Government and Politics, 1800–1850." *To Preserve and Defend: Essays on Kingston in the Nineteenth Century.* Gerald Turchinsky ed. Montreal : McGill-Queen's University Press, 1976.

Blackwell, John D. "Crime in the London District, 1828–1837: A Case Study of the Effect of the 1833 Reform in Upper Canadian Penal Law." *Historical Essays on Upper Canada: New Perspectives.* JK Johnson and Bruce G. Wilson eds. Ottawa: Carleton University Press, 1989.

Bleasdale, Ruth. "Class Conflict on the Canals of Upper Canada in the 1840s." *Labour/Le Travail,* 7 (Spring 1981), 9–39.

Burkholder, Ruth M. "Records of the Courts of the Quarter Sessions of the Peace." *Families* 32 No. 1 (1993).

Burkholder, Ruth M. "Criminal Assize Clerk: Indictment Case Files 1853–1929." *Families* 34 No. 1 (1995).

Craven, Paul. "Law and Ideology: The Toronto Police Court." *Essays in the History of Canadian Law*, Volume II, David H. Flaherty ed. Toronto: University of Toronto Press for the Osgoode Society, 1983.

Crawford, K. G. *Canadian Municipal Government.* Toronto: University of Toronto Press, 1954.

Croft, William F. "Sidelights on the Hamilton Police Force." *Wentworth Bygones* 7 (1967), 64–66.

Cross, Michael. "The Shiner's War: Social Violence in the Ottawa Valley in the 1830s." *Canadian Historical Review* 54 (1973), 1–26.

Elliott, John K. "Crime and Punishment in Early Upper Canada." *Ontario Historical Society Papers and Records* 27 (1931), 335–40.

Fraser, Robert ed. *Provincial Justice: Upper Canadian Legal Portraits.* Toronto: University of Toronto Press, 1992.

Friedland, Martin L. *Sentencing Structure in Canada: Historical Perspectives.* Ottawa: Deptartment of Justice Canada, Research and Development Directorate, Policy, Programs and Research Branch, 1988.

Glazebrook, G. P. de T. *Life in Ontario: A Social History.* Toronto: University of Toronto Press, 1975.

Golz, Annalee. "Uncovering and Reconstructing Family Violence in Ontario Criminal Case Files." *On the Case: Explorations in Social History.* Franca Iacovetta and Wendy Michinson eds. Toronto: University of Toronto Press, 1988.

Gourlay, Robert. *Statistical Account of Upper Canada.* London: Simpkin and Marshall, 1832.

History of the County of Middlesex, Canada. Toronto and London: W.A. and C.L. Godspeed, 1889; Reprint Belleville, ON: Mika Studio, 1972.

Houston, Susan E. "Politics, Schools, and Social Change in Upper Canada." *Canadian Historical Review* 53 No. 3 (Sept 1972), 249–71.

Jameson, Anna. *Winter Studies and Summer Rambles in Canada.* London: Saunders and Otley, 1838.

Johnson, J.K. "The Social Composition of the Toronto Bank Guards, 1837–1838." *Ontario History* 64 (1972), 95–104.

Johnson, J.K. *Becoming Prominent: Regional Leadership in Upper Canada, 1791–1841.* Kingston, ON: McGill-Queen's University Press, 1989.

Jones, James Edmund. *Pioneer Crimes and Punishments in Toronto and the Home District.* Toronto: George N. Morang, 1924.

Keele, W.C. "*A Brief View of the Township Laws up to the Present Time: With a Treatise on the Law and Office of Constable, the Law Relative to Landlord and Tenant, Distress for Rent, Innkeepers, etc.*" Toronto: W.J. Coates CIHM 10787, 1835, 1884.

Kilbourn, William. *The Firebrand: William Lyon Mackenzie and the Rebellion in Upper Canada.* Toronto: Dundurn Press, 2008.

Lacey, E.A. "The Trials of John Montgomery." *Ontario History* 52 No. 3 (Sept 1960), 141–58.

Lewthwaite, Susan. "Violence, Law and Community in Rural Upper Canada." *Essays in the History of Canadian Law,* Volume V. Jim Phillips, Tina Loo, and Susan Lewthwaite eds. Toronto: University of Toronto Press for the Osgoode Society, 1983.

Mackenzie, William, "Report on the Condition of the Prisoners in York Gaol," Upper Canada, House of Assembly, *Journals*, 1830, Appendix, 162.

MacRae, Marion and Anthony Adamson. *Cornerstones of Order: Courthouses and Town Halls Of Ontario, 1784–1914*. Toronto: The Osgoode Society, Clarke, Irwin, 1983.

Malcolmson, Patricia E. "The Poor in Kingston, 1815–1850." *To Preserve and Defend: Essays on Kingston in the Nineteenth Century*. Gerald Turchinsky ed. Montreal: McGill-Queen's University Press, 1976, 281–97.

Manson, Allan. *Sentencing and Penal Policy in Canada: Cases, Materials, and Commentary*. Toronto: Emond Montgomery Publications, 2008.

Marks, Lynne. "Christian Harmony Family, Neighbours and Community in Upper Canadian Church discipline Records." *On the Case: Explorations in Social History*, Franca Iacovetta and Wendy Michinson eds. Toronto: University of Toronto Press, 1988.

McCormick, Chris and Len Green, eds. *Crime and Deviance in Canada: Historical Perspectives*. Toronto: Canadian Scholars' Press, 2005.

McKenna, Katherine M.J. "Women's Agency in Upper Canada: Prescott Board of Police Record, 1834–1850." *Histoire Sociale / Social History* 36 No. 72 (2003), 347–70.

Mills, David. *The Idea of Loyalty in Upper Canada, 1784–1850*. Kingston, ON, and Montreal: McGill-Queen's University Press, 1988.

Moore, Christopher. *The Law Society of Upper Canada and Ontario's Lawyers, 1797–1997*. Toronto: University of Toronto Press, 1997.

Mosser, Christine, ed. *York, Upper Canada Minutes of Town Meetings and Lists of Inhabitants 1797–1823*. Toronto: Metropolitan Toronto Library Board, 1984.

Murray, David. *Colonial Justice: Justice, Morality, and Crime in the Niagara District, 1791–1849*. Toronto: University of Toronto Press, 2002.

Oliver, Peter. *Terror to Evil-Doers: Prisons and Punishments in Nineteenth-Century Ontario*. Toronto: University of Toronto Press, 1998.

Oliver, Peter. "From Jails to Penitentiary: The Demise of Community Corrections in Early Ontario." *Correctional Options* 4 (1984), 1–10.

Phelan, Josephine. "The Tar and Feather Case, Gore Assizes, August 1827." *Ontario History* 68 No. 1 (1976), 17–23.

Riddell, William Renwick. "The 'Ordinary' Court of Chancery in Upper Canada: An Attempt by the Lieutenant-Governor to Act as

Chancellor." *Ontario History* 22 (1925), 222–38.

Riddell, William Renwick. "The Courts of Ontario." *University of Pennsylvania Law Review and American Law Register,* 62 No. 1 (Nov 1913), 17–33.

Riddell, William Renwick. "A Criminal Circuit in Upper Canada a Century Ago." *Journal of the American Institute of Criminal Law and Criminology* 12 No. 1 (1921), 91–104.

Riddell, William Renwick. "Judges in the Executive Council of Upper Canada." *Michigan Law Review* 20 No. 7 (May 1922), 716–36.

Riddell, William Renwick. "Criminal Courts and Law in Early (Upper) Canada." *Ontario Historical Society Papers and Records* 22 (1925).

Rogers, Nicholas. "Serving Toronto the Good: The Development of the City Police Force 1834–84." *Forging a Consensus: Historical Essays on Toronto.* Victor Loring Russell ed. Toronto: University of Toronto Press, 1984, 116–40.

Romney, Paul. "The Ordeal of William Higgins." *Ontario History* 67 No. 2 (1975), 69–89.

Romney, Paul. "Rebel as Magistrate: William Lyon Mackenzie and His Enemies." *Essays in the History of Canadian Law,* Volume V. Jim Phillips, Tina Loo, and Susan Lewthwaite eds. Toronto: University of Toronto Press for the Osgoode Society, 1983.

Romney, Paul. "A Struggle for Authority: Toronto Society and Politics in 1834." *Forging a Consensus: Historical Essays on Toronto.* Victor Loring Russell ed. Toronto: University of Toronto Press, 1984, 9–40.

Romney, Paul. *Mr. Attorney: The Attorney General for Ontario in Court, Cabinet, and Legislature 1791–1899.* Toronto: University of Toronto Press, 1986.

Romney, Paul. "From the Types Riot to Rebellion: Elite Ideology, Antilegal Sentiment, Political Violence, and the Rule of Law in Upper Canada." *Ontario History* 79 No. 2 (1987), 113–44.

Romney, Paul. "Very Late Loyalist Fantasies: Nostalgic Tory 'History' and the Rule of Law in Upper Canada." *Canadian Perspectives on Law and Society: Essays in Legal History.* W. Wesley Pue and J.B. Wright eds. Ottawa: Carleton University Press, October, 1988, 119–47.

Romney, Paul. *The Administration of Justice in Ontario 1784–1900.* Winnipeg: University of Manitoba, Faculty of Law, Canadian Legal History Project, 1991.

Romney, Paul. "Upper Canada (Ontario): The Administration of Justice, 1784–1850." *Manitoba Law Journal* 23 No. 1-2 (1996), 183–213.

Smandych, Russell C. "Beware of the 'Evil American Monster': Upper Canadian Views on the Need for a Penitentiary, 1830–1834." *Canadian Journal of Criminology* 33 No. 2 (1991), 125–47.

Smith, W.L. *The Pioneers of Old Ontario.* Toronto: George N. Morang, 1923.

Strange, Carolyn. *Imposing Goodness: Crime and Justice in "Toronto the Good," 1793–1953.* Toronto: Law Society of Upper Canada, 1991. (Publication to accompany a Market Gallery exhibit.)

Talbot, Charles K. *Justice in Early Ontario, 1791–1840.* Ottawa: Crimcare Publications, 1983.

Torrance, Gordon V. "The History of Law Enforcement in Hamilton from 1833 to 1967." *Wentworth Bygones* 7 (1967), 67–72.

Vronsky, Peter. "History of the Toronto Police." *www.russianbooks.org/crime/cp0.htm* (accessed 2 March 2009).

Weaver, John C. *Crimes, Constables and Courts: Order and Transgression in a Canadian City, 1816–1870.* Montreal and Kingston: McGill-Queen's University Press, 1995.

Weaver, John. "Crime, Public Order, and Repression: The Gore District in Upheaval, 1832–1851." *Ontario History* 78 No. 3 (September 1986).

Wilson, W.R. "The Legislature and Early Legislation in Upper Canada." *Historical Narratives of Early Canada, www.uppercanadahistory.ca* (accessed September 2009).

Wilton, Carol. "'A Firebrand Amongst the People': The Durham Meetings and Popular Politics in Upper Canada." *Canadian Historical Review* 75 No. 3 (1994), 346–75.

Wilton, Carol. "'Lawless Law': Conservative Political Violence in Upper Canada, 1818–41." *Law and History Review* 13 No. 1 (1995), 111–36.

Wise, S.F. "Upper Canada and the Conservative Tradition." *Profiles of a Province: Studies in the History of Ontario.* Edith G. Firth ed. Toronto: Ontario Historical Society, 1967, 20–33.

Wright, Barry. "Sedition in Upper Canada: Contested Legality." *Labour/Le Travail* 29 (Spring 1992), 7–57.

NOTES

Chapter 1

1. J. M. Beattie, *Attitudes Toward Crime and Punishment in Upper Canada 1830–1850: A Documentary Study* (Toronto: Working Paper of the Centre of Criminology, University of Toronto, 1977), 1.

2. Christine Mosser ed., *York, Upper Canada Minutes of Town Meetings and Lists of Inhabitants 1797–1823* (Toronto: Metropolitan Toronto Library Board, 1984).

3. David Mills, *The Idea of Loyalty in Upper Canada, 1784–1850* (Kingston and Montreal: McGill-Queen's University Press, 1988), 5.

4. *Ibid.*, 18.

5. S. F Wise, "Upper Canada and the Conservative Tradition," *Profiles of a Province: Studies in the History of Ontario*, Edith G. Firth ed. (Toronto: Ontario Historical Society, 1967), 20, 31.

6. *Ibid.*

7. See Chapter V for a discussion of political repression and dissent.

8. Mills, *The Idea of Loyalty*, 12.

9. David Murray, *Colonial Justice: Justice, Morality, and Crime in the Niagara District, 1791–1849* (Toronto: University of Toronto Press, 2002), 23.

10. G. Blaine Baker, "'So Elegant a Web': Providential Order and the Rule of Secular Law in Early Nineteenth-Century Upper Canada,"

University of Toronto Law Journal 38, No. 2 (1988); Paul Romney, "From the Types Riot to Rebellion: Elite Ideology, Anti-legal Sentiment, Political Violence, and the Rule of Law in Upper Canada," *Ontario History*, 79 No. 2 (1987), 135–36.

11. George Sheppard, *Plunder, Profit and Paroles: A Social History of the War of 1812 in Upper Canada* (Montreal and Kingston: McGill-Queen's Press, 1994), 13, 18.

12. Statistics Canada. UC Table III — Birth Places of the People, 1842 — Upper Canada (table), 1842 — Census of Upper Canada (database), using E-STAT (distributor), *estat.statcan.gc.ca/cgi-win/cnsmcgi.exe?Lang=E&EST-Fi=EStat\English\SC_RR-eng.htm* (accessed: 19 May 2010).

13. Statistics Canada. UC Table II — Population by Religions, 1842 — Upper Canada (table), 1842 — Census of Upper Canada (database), using E-STAT (distributor), *estat.statcan.gc.ca/cgi-win/cnsmcgi.exe?Lang=E&EST-Fi=EStat\English\SC_RR-eng.htm* (accessed: 19 May 2010).

14. J. Jerald Bellomo, "Upper Canadian Attitudes Towards Crime and Punishment (1832–1851)," *Ontario History* 64, No. 2 (1972), 12.

15. *Ibid.*, 12–13.

16. Bellomo, "Upper Canadian Attitudes," 13–16; Beattie, *Attitudes Toward Crime and Punishment in Upper Canada 1830–1850: A Documentary Study* (Toronto: Working Paper of the Centre of Criminology, University of Toronto, 1977), 2–5.

17. Beattie, *Attitudes toward Crime and Punishment in Upper Canada 1830–1850: A Documentary Study*, 3–4.

18. James Edmund Jones, *Pioneer Crimes and Punishments in Toronto and the Home District* (Toronto: George N. Morang, 1924), 169.

19. Beattie, *Attitudes toward Crime and Punishment in Upper Canada 1830–1850: A Documentary Study*, 6–35.

20. This is an estimate based on the report that there were fifty families in Toronto in 1837; Murray, *Colonial Justice: Justice, Morality, and Crime in the Niagara District, 1791–1849*, 158–60.

21. *British Colonist*, 19 Jan 1842, Page 3, Column 2, originally from the *Brantford Courier*.

22. Bellomo, "Upper Canadian Attitudes," 11.

23. John C. Weaver, *Crimes, Constables and Courts: Order and Transgres-*

sion in a Canadian City, 1816–1870 (Montreal & Kingston: McGill-Queen's University Press, 1995), 53.

24. Weaver, *Crimes, Constables and Courts*, 53–54; John Weaver, "Crime, Public Order, and Repression: The Gore District in Upheaval, 1832–1851," *Ontario History* 78 No. 3 (September 1986), 191–94.

25. Weaver, "Crime, Public Order, and Repression: The Gore District in Upheaval, 1832–1851," 191.

26. Constance Backhouse, *Petticoats and Prejudice: Women and the Law in Nineteenth Century Canada* (Toronto: Women's Press, 1991), 178.

27. *The Colonial Advocate*, 17 April 1834, Page 2 citing the *Family Journal*.

28. *An Act to Reduce the Number of Cases in Which Capital Punishment May Be Inflicted...* Statutes of Upper Canada, 3 Wm. IV (1833) c. 4 [prior to 1833, capital crimes included counterfeiting, forgery, killing or maiming cattle, burning a stack of corn, straw, hay, or wood, destroying woollen goods in the loom, and impersonating a pensioner, among a great many others].

29. Murray, *Colonial Justice: Justice, Morality, and Crime in the Niagara District, 1791–1849*, 136–38.

30. Weaver, "Crime, Public Order, and Repression," 180; This includes only those crimes where offenders were committed to gaol.

31. Murray, *Colonial Justice: Justice, Morality, and Crime in the Niagara District, 1791–1849*, 135–37.

32. *Ibid.*, 136.

33. "Minutes of the Court of General Quarter Sessions of the Peace for the London District..." in *Twenty-Second Report of the Department of Public Records and Archives of Ontario*, 1933, 185, 186, 189, 193, 194.

34. Jones, *Pioneer crimes and punishments*, 37–46.

35. Murray, *Colonial Justice: Justice, Morality, and Crime in the Niagara District, 1791–1849*, 137–38.

36. *Ibid.*, 139.

37. See appendix for information about relative values.

38. Murray, *Colonial Justice: Justice, Morality, and Crime in the Niagara District, 1791–1849*, 139, citing King vs. Samuel Farensworth, Oct. 1836, RG 22 Series 372, Box 25 File 22, Archives of Ontario.

39. *An Act to Reduce the Number of Cases in Which Capital Punishment May Be Inflicted...* Statutes of Upper Canada, 3 William IV (1833). c. 4, s. 6.

40. *An Act for Consolidating and Amending the Statutes in this Province Relative to Offences Against the Person*, Statutes of Canada, 4, 5 Victoria (1841), c. 27, s. 17.
41. Murray, *Colonial Justice: Justice, Morality, and Crime in the Niagara District, 1791–1849*, 158–60.
42. *Ibid.*, 141.
43. *Ibid.*, 140.
44. *Ibid.*, 141.
45. Weaver, "Crime, Public Order, and Repression," 180. This includes only those crimes where offenders were committed to gaol.
46. Statutes of Quebec, 29 George III, (1788/1789), c. 3.
47. W. R. Riddell "Criminal Courts and Law in Early (Upper) Canada," *Ontario Historical Society Papers and Records*, 22 (1925), citing *Blackstone' Commentaries*, Book IV, 229, and Statutes of Quebec, 29 George III, (1789), c. 3.
48. Murray, *Colonial Justice: Justice, Morality, and Crime in the Niagara District, 1791–1849*, 140.
49. *Ibid.*, 141; Riddell "Criminal Courts and Law," citing 7 William IV (1826/1827), c.4.
50. The average rate of crimes against public order in the Gore District between 1832 and 1840 was 33 per 100,000 according to Weaver, "Crime, Public Order, and Repression," 180. This includes only those crimes where offenders were committed to gaol.
51. G. P. de T. Glazebrook, *Life in Ontario: A Social History* (Toronto: University of Toronto Press, 1975), 99.
52. Weaver, "Crime, Public Order, and Repression."
53. Murray, *Colonial Justice: Justice, Morality, and Crime in the Niagara District, 1791–1849*, 143.
54. *Colonial Advocate*, 22 May 1834, 12 June 1834, 26 June 1834.
55. Murray, *Colonial Justice: Justice, Morality, and Crime in the Niagara District, 1791–1849*, 147.
56. "City Police Report," *Advocate*, 12 June 1834, 3.
57. Barry Wright, "Sedition in Upper Canada: Contested Legality," *Labour/Le Travail* 29 (Spring 1992), 8.
58. *Ibid.*, 9.
59. H. P. Gundy, "Francis Collins," *Canadian Dictionary of Biography*, Vol. 6, 164–65.

Chapter Two

1. See Chapter Six for a full discussion of the role of Magistrate/Justice of the Peace and records pertaining to this office.

2. Peter Oliver, *Terror to Evil-Doers: Prisons and Punishments in Nineteenth-Century Ontario* (Toronto: University of Toronto Press, 1998), 11.

3. Paul Romney, *The Administration of Justice in Ontario 1784–1900* (Winnipeg : University of Manitoba, Faculty of Law, Canadian Legal History Project, 1991), 20–21; Murray, *Colonial Justice: Justice, Morality, and Crime in the Niagara District, 1791–1849*, 26–28, 39.

4. See Chapter Six for a full discussion of the role of the Sheriff and records pertaining to this office.

5. See Chapter Six for a full discussion of the role of the Constable and records pertaining to this office.

6. Archives Descriptive Database, Archives of Ontario.

7. Murray, *Colonial Justice: Justice, Morality, and Crime in the Niagara District, 1791–1849 (Toronto: University of Toronto Press, 2002)*, 66–70.

8. Jones, *Pioneer Crimes and Punishments*, 150.

9. Lynn Marks, "Christian Harmony Family, Neighbours and Community in Upper Canadian Church discipline Records," *On the Case: Explorations in Social History*, Franca Iacovetta and Wendy Michinson eds. (Toronto: University of Toronto Press, 1988).

10. *Ibid.*, 120–21, citing Woodstock Baptist Church minutes, 13 March 1841, Family History Archives, Victoria.

11. If the victim was a woman, her husband, brother, or father would usually make the report. In the case of a child the report would be made by the father.

12. David Murray, *Colonial Justice: Justice, Morality, and Crime in the Niagara District, 1791–1849* (Toronto: University of Toronto Press, 2002), 139.

13. See Chapter Six for a full discussion of the role of the Coroner's Jury and relevant records.

14. Susan Lewthwaite, "Violence, Law and Community in Rural Upper Canada," *Essays in the History of Canadian Law*, Volume V, Jim Phillips, Tina Loo, and Susan Lewthwaite eds. (Toronto: University of Toronto Press, 1983), 367, citing Case Files, Newcastle District Court of General Quarter Sessions of the Peace, RG 22 Series 31, Archives of Ontario.

15. Murray, *Colonial Justice: Justice, Morality, and Crime in the Niagara District, 1791–1849*, 70, citing King vs. Barney Woolman, March 1834, Lincoln County Court of General Quarter Sessions of the Peace Records, Box 16 File 55, RG 22 Series 372, Archives of Ontario.

16. *Ibid.*, 71–72, citing Frances Ann Thompson, "Local Authority and District Autonomy: The Niagara Magistracy and Constabulary," PhD thesis, University of Ottawa, 1996.

Chapter Three

1. Weaver, *Crimes, Constables and Courts*, 29.

2. W. C. Keele, *A Brief View of the Township Laws Up To the Present Time: With a Treatise on the Law and Office of Constable, the Law Relative to Landlord and Tenant, Distress for Rent, Innkeepers, etc.* (Toronto? : 1835, 1884) (Toronto: W. J. Coates CIHM 10787), 107–109; *An Act to Provide for the Summary Punishment of Petty Trespasses and other Offences, 4 William IV* (1834), c.4.

3. William Renwick Riddell, "The Courts of Ontario," *University of Pennsylvania Law Review and American Law Register*, 62 No. 1 (Nov 1913), 29–31; Keele, *A Brief View of the Township Laws Up To the Present Time: With a Treatise on the Law and Office of Constable, the Law Relative to Landlord and Tenant, Distress for Rent, Innkeepers, etc.*, 107–109; Murray, *Colonial Justice: Justice, Morality, and Crime in the Niagara District, 1791–1849 (Toronto: University of Toronto Press, 2002)*, 81, 135; Lewthwaite, "Violence, Law and Community," *Essays in the History of Canadian Law*, Volume V, Jim Phillips, Tina Loo, and Susan Lewthwaite eds. (Toronto: University of Toronto Press, 1983), 375–76; *An Act to Provide for the Summary Punishment of Petty Trespasses and other Offences, 4 William IV* (1834), c.4.

4. Keele, *A Brief View of the Township Laws Up To the Present Time: With a Treatise on the Law and Office of Constable, the Law Relative to Landlord and Tenant, Distress for Rent, Innkeepers, etc.*, 107–109; *An Act to provide for the Summary Punishment of Petty Trespasses and other Offences, 4 William IV* (1834), c.4.

5. Murray, *Colonial Justice: Justice, Morality, and Crime in the Niagara District, 1791–1849*, 147; Keele, *A Brief View of the Township Laws Up To the Present Time: With a Treatise on the Law and Office of Constable, the Law Relative to Landlord and Tenant, Distress for Rent, Innkeepers,*

etc., 107–109; *An Act to provide for the Summary Punishment of Petty Trespasses and other Offences, 4 William IV* (1834), c.4.

6. Weaver, *Crimes, Constables and Courts*, 29–31; *An Act to provide for the Summary Punishment of Petty Trespasses and other Offences, 4 William IV* (1834), c.4.

7. Lewthwaite, "Violence, Law and Community," 380, citing examples from the Informations Book of D.B. Stephenson (a Justice of the Peace), Miscellaneous Records, 1834–1839, Prince Edward County Court of General Sessions of the Peace, RG 22 Series 86, Archives of Ontario; Murray, *Colonial Justice: Justice, Morality, and Crime in the Niagara District, 1791–1849*, citing several cases in the files of Alexander Hamilton of Queenston, where his concluding remark is "compromised," King vs. Edward Walker, 26 October 1829, Hamilton Papers, MS 24 I26 Volume 44, Library and Archives Canada.

8. Murray, *Colonial Justice: Justice, Morality, and Crime in the Niagara District, 1791–1849*, 41, citing Boulton to Charles Richardson, 14 July 1830, Lincoln County Court of General Quarter Sessions of the Peace Records, RG 22 Series 372, Box 7 File 2, Archives of Ontario.

9. Lewthwaite, "Violence, Law and Community," 365–66.

10. The court is also occasionally mentioned in the city council journals and there was one formal report in the *Journals of the Legislative Assembly*, 4–5, Victoria (1841), Appendix S, Appendix C.

11. Katherine M. J. McKenna, "Women's Agency in Upper Canada: Prescott Board of Police Record, 1834–1850," *Histoire Sociale /Social History* 36, No. 72 (2003), 353; City of Toronto Archives collections description for City of Toronto Mayor's Court, Fonds 95.

12. Frederick H. Armstrong, *Handbook of Upper Canadian Chronology*, revised edition, (Toronto: Dundurn Press, 1985), 201; Brockville, for example: *An Act to establish a Police in the Town of Brockville, in the District of Johnstown*, Statutes of Upper Canada, 2 William IV (1832), c. 17.

13. George Betts, "Municipal Government and Politics, 1800–1850," *To Preserve and Defend*, Gerald Turchinsky ed. (Montreal: McGill-Queen's University Press, 1976), 230; K.G. Crawford, *Canadian Municipal Government* (Toronto: University of Toronto Press, 1954), 26; *An Act to Extend the Limits of the Town of York; to Erect the Said Town Into a City; and to Incorporate it Under the Name of the City of Toronto*, Statutes of Upper Canada, 4 William IV (1834) c. 23.

14. McKenna, "Women's Agency in Upper Canada," 356, citing the Prescott Board of Police minutes of 7 September 1841.

15. *Ibid.*, 354, 356.

16. *Ibid.*, 351–54.

17. *Ibid.*, 348.

18. *An Act establishing Trial by Jury in Upper Canada*, Statutes of Upper Canada, 32 George III (1792), c. 2.

19. Anna Jameson, *Winter Studies and Summer Rambles in Canada* (London: Saunders and Otley, 1838),Vol. 1, 256–57.

20. "Charge to the Gentlemen of the Grand Jury," 9 August 1825, Cornwall, unbound legal notebooks, William Dummer Powell papers, L16, Baldwin Room, Toronto Public Library.

21. Murray, *Colonial Justice: Justice, Morality, and Crime in the Niagara District, 1791–1849*; Weaver, *Crimes, Constables and Courts*, 33–34.

22. Murray, *Colonial Justice: Justice, Morality, and Crime in the Niagara District, 1791–1849*, 70.

23. *Ibid.*, 139.

24. "Minutes of the Court of General Quarter Sessions of the peace for the Home District..." *Twenty-First Report of the Department of Public Records and Archives of Ontario*, (1932), 14, 25, 27–28, 74, 96, 99.

25. Romney, *The Administration of Justice in Ontario 1784–1900* (Winnipeg: University of Manitoba, Faculty of Law, Canadian Legal History Project, 1991), 14.

26. Weaver, *Crimes, Constables and Courts*, 53.

27. *Ibid.*, 36–37.

28. Murray, *Colonial Justice: Justice, Morality, and Crime in the Niagara District, 1791–1849*, 70–71.

29. *Ibid.*, 28.

30. R vs. Charles Ragan, 15 January 1835, Minutes, Western District/Essex County Court of General Quarter Sessions of the Peace, RG 22-103,Volume 2, Archive of Ontario MS 166 Reel 1.

31. Information and Complaint of Carson Mosier, 11 January 1835, Criminal Case Files, Western District Court of General Quarter Sessions of the Peace, RG 22-109, pages 1080–81, Archives of Ontario, MS 205, Reel 2.

32. Evidence (Deposition) of William Spackman, 12 January 1835, Criminal Case Files, Western District Court of General Quarter

Sessions of the Peace, RG 22-109, pages 1077–79, Archives of Ontario, MS 205, Reel 2.

33. Evidence of Almira Akerley, 12 January 1835, Criminal Case Files, Western District Court of General Quarter Sessions of the Peace, RG 22-109, pages 1075–76, Archives of Ontario, MS 205, Reel 2.

34. Examination of Charles Ragan, 12 January 1835, Criminal Case Files, Western District Court of General Quarter Sessions of the Peace, RG 22-109, pages 1073–74, Archives of Ontario, MS 205, Reel 2.

35. Recognizance of John Jones, Caleb Akerley and William Spackman, 12 January 1835, Criminal Case Files, Western District Court of General Quarter Sessions of the Peace, RG 22-109, pages 1069–70, Archives of Ontario, MS 205, Reel 2; Recognizance of Almira Akerley, 12 January 1835, Criminal Case Files, Western District Court of General Quarter Sessions of the Peace, RG 22-109, pages 1071–72, Archives of Ontario, MS 205, Reel 2.

36. Indictment of Charles Ragan, filed 14 January 1835, Criminal Case Files, Western District Court of General Quarter Sessions of the Peace, RG 22-109, pages 1067–68, Archives of Ontario, MS 205, Reel 2.

37. City of Toronto Mayor's Court Proceedings, RG7 Series E, City of Toronto Archives.

38. Paul Romney, "A Struggle for Authority: Toronto Society and Politics in 1834," *Forging a Consensus: Historical Essays on Toronto*, Victor Loring Russell ed. (Toronto: University of Toronto Press, 1984), 24–25, citing Proceedings of the Mayor's Court, 2 June, 3 June, 1834, RG 7 E (Now Fonds 95, Series 507), City of Toronto Archives; *Advocate* 5, 12, June and 10 July; *Canadian Correspondent*, 12 July 1834; *Patriot*, June and July 1834.

39. These can be found in the Upper Canada Sundries (RG5 A1, Library and Archives Canada).

40. R. v Henry Sovereen, Minutes of the London District Assize, 8 July 1832, Archives of Ontario, RG 22-134.

41. R. vs. Sovereen, London District, August 1832, Bench book of James Buchanan MacAulay, RG 22-390-1 Box 2, Archives of Ontario.

Chapter Four

1. Oliver, *Terror to Evil-Doers: Prisons and Punishments in Nineteenth-Century Ontario* (Toronto: University of Toronto Press, 1998), 3–4.

2. *Ibid.*,13.

3. *Ibid.*

4. *Ibid.*, xx, xxi.

5. Statement of George Bradshaw and Jacob Misner, Wainfeet Town Wardens, 3 December 1838; deposition of Elizabeth Cochrane, 29 March 1839, RG22-372, Box 34 File 8, Archives of Ontario, cited in David Murray, *Colonial Justice: Justice, Morality, and Crime in the Niagara District, 1791–1849 (Toronto: University of Toronto Press, 2002)*, 159.

6. Murray, *Colonial Justice: Justice, Morality, and Crime in the Niagara District, 1791–1849*, 159–60.

7. Oliver, *Terror to Evil-Doers: Prisons and Punishments in Nineteenth-Century Ontario*, 13.

8. See appendix for an explanation of my calculations of worth in today's terms.

9. Lewthwaite, "Violence, Law and Community," *Essays in the History of Canadian Law*, Volume V, Jim Phillips, Tina Loo, and Susan Lewthwaite eds. (Toronto: University of Toronto Press, 1983), 356–57, citing RG8-23, box 1, file "January 8, 1840," Archives of Ontario.

10. Jones, *Pioneer crimes and punishments*, 2.

11. *Ibid.*,18, citing 2 Cor 11: 24.

12. Oliver, *Terror to Evil-Doers: Prisons and Punishments in Nineteenth-Century Ontario*, 20–21; Murray, *Colonial Justice: Justice, Morality, and Crime in the Niagara District, 1791–1849*, 140.

13. Peter Oliver, "From Jails to Penitentiary: The Demise of Community Corrections in Early Ontario," *Correctional Options* 4 (1984).

14. Oliver, *Terror to Evil-Doers: Prisons and Punishments in Nineteenth-Century Ontario*, 24–25; Murray, *Colonial Justice: Justice, Morality, and Crime in the Niagara District, 1791–1849*, 140; An *Act for Improving the Administration of Criminal Justice in this Province*, Statutes of Canada 4, 5 Victoria (1841) c. 24, s. 31.

15. Murray, *Colonial Justice: Justice, Morality, and Crime in the Niagara District, 1791–1849*, 140.

16. *History of the County of Middlesex, Canada* (Toronto & London: W.A. and C.L. Godspeed, 1889), Reprint: Belleville, ON: Mika Studio, 1972, 124.

17. Jones, *Pioneer crimes and punishments*, 28–29.

18. *History of the County of Middlesex*, 127.

19. Oliver, *Terror to Evil-Doers: Prisons and Punishments in Nineteenth-Century Ontario*, 25–26; Jones, *Pioneer crimes and punishments*, 15, 26–27.

20. King vs. Charlotte Lee, 2 June 1834, Proceedings of the (Toronto) Mayor's Court, RG7 E box 1, file 1, City of Toronto Archives; "The Mayor's Court," the *Advocate*, 12 June 1834, Page 1, Column 5.

21. "The Mayor's Court," the *Advocate*, 12 June 1834, 1–2.

22. William Kilbourn, *The Firebrand: William Lyon Mackenzie and the Rebellion in Upper Canada* (Toronto: Dundurn Press, 2008).

23. Oliver, *Terror to Evil-Doers: Prisons and Punishments in Nineteenth-Century Ontario*, 29–34.

24. Weaver, *Crimes, Constables and Courts*, 24–25.

25. Blackwell, "Crime in the London District, 1828–1837," 576.

26. *Ibid.*, 567–71, citing *An Act to Reduce the Number of Cases in Which Capital Punishment May Be Inflicted…* Statutes of Upper Canada 3 William IV (1833), c. 4.

27. *An Act for Consolidating and Amending the Statutes in this Province Relative to Offences Against the Person*, Statutes of Canada, 4,5 Victoria (1841), c. 27.

28. Oliver, *Terror to Evil-Doers: Prisons and Punishments in Nineteenth-Century Ontario*, 29–34.

29. Weaver, "Crime, Public Order, and Repression," 203.

30. Martin L. Friedland, *Sentencing Structure in Canada: Historical Perspectives*. (Ottawa: Deptartment of Justice Canada, Research and Development Directorate, Policy, Programs and Research Branch, 1988) 5; Charles K. Talbot, *Justice in Early Ontario, 1791–1840*. (Ottawa: Crimcare Publications, 1983), 145–49; Beattie, *Attitudes Toward Crime and Punishment in Upper Canada 1830–1850: A Documentary Study* (Toronto: Working Paper of the Centre of Criminology, University of Toronto, 1977), 9, 57, 65–67.

31. Oliver, *Terror to Evil-Doers: Prisons and Punishments in Nineteenth-Century Ontario*, 4–6.

32. *Ibid.*, 10.
33. *Ibid.*, 7–10.
34. *Ibid.*, 11.
35. *Ibid.*, 12.
36. *Ibid.*, 5.
37. Weaver, *Crimes, Constables and Courts*, 60; Oliver, *Terror to Evil-Doers: Prisons and Punishments in Nineteenth-Century Ontario*, 6, 9.
38. Murray, *Colonial Justice: Justice, Morality, and Crime in the Niagara District, 1791–1849*, 90–97, 103.
39. *Ibid.*
40. Jones, *Pioneer Crimes and Punishments*, 75–85.
41. Murray, *Colonial Justice: Justice, Morality, and Crime in the Niagara District, 1791–1849*, 91–98, citing Autopsy report of Henry Rolls, 23 March 1841, jail records, Lincoln County Court of General Quarter Sessions of the Peace Records, RG 22 Series 372, Box 41 File 24, Archives of Ontario.
42. Jones, *Pioneer Crimes and Punishments*, 37.
43. Oliver, *Terror to Evil-Doers: Prisons and Punishments in Nineteenth-Century Ontario*, 49; Robert Gourlay, *Statistical Account of Upper Canada* (London: Simpkin and Marshall, 1832).
44. Oliver, *Terror to Evil-Doers: Prisons and Punishments in Nineteenth-Century Ontario*, 55.
45. S.R. Mealing, "William Dummer Powell," *Dictionary of Canadian Biography*, citing an 1827 survey of the province's eleven district jails.
46. *Ibid.*, 48.
47. *Ibid.*, 8.
48. Weaver, *Crimes, Constables and Courts*, 59.
49. Talbot, *Justice in Early Ontario*, 286.
50. Jones, *Pioneer Crimes and Punishments*, 51.
51. *Ibid.*, 57–67.
52. *Ibid.*, 70–72.
53. *Ibid.*, 99–100.
54. Oliver, *Terror to Evil-Doers: Prisons and Punishments in Nineteenth-Century Ontario*, 35.
55. *Ibid.*, 36–38, citing Upper Canada Sundries (LAC RG 5 A1, 8 July 1834).
56. William Lyon Mackenzie, "Report on the Condition of the Pris-

oners in York Gaol," Upper Canada, House of Assembly, *Journals*, 1830, Appendix, 162.

57. Oliver, *Terror to Evil-Doers: Prisons and Punishments in Nineteenth-Century Ontario*, 81.

58. *Ibid.*, 82–83.

59. *Ibid.*, 82–83.

60. *Ibid.*, 106.

61. Bellomo, "Upper Canadian Attitudes," 16.

62. *Ibid.*, 16–17.

63. Russell C. Smandych, "Beware of the 'Evil American Monster': Upper Canadian Views on the Need for a Penitentiary, 1830–1834," *Canadian Journal of Criminology* 33, No. 2 (1991): 137.

64. Oliver, *Terror to Evil-Doers: Prisons and Punishments in Nineteenth-Century Ontario*.

65. *Ibid.*, 106.

66. *Ibid.*, 119–20.

67. *Ibid.*, 122–23.

68. *Ibid.*, 152.

69. Weaver, *Crimes, Constables and Courts*, 53.

Chapter Five

1. Untitled article beginning, "A singular and rather obsolete kind of legal inquiry…" the *British Whig*, 12 September 1837, page 3, column 2; untitled article beginning "The Assizes for the Midland District…," the *British Whig*, 28 September 1837, page 3 column 2; "Assizes for the Midland District," the *British Whig*, 7 October 1837, page 3, columns 1–3.

2. "Horrible and Brutal Execution," the *British Whig*, 1 December 1837, page 3, columns 4–5; "The Atrocious Execution," the *British Whig*, 8 December 1837, page 3, columns 2–3.

3. "The Assizes," the *Upper Canada Herald*, 10 October 1837, page 2, column 4.

4. "The Midland District Assizes," the *Chronicle & Gazette*, 11 October 1837, page 2, column 3; "The Execution," the *Chronicle*, 2 December 1837, page 2, column 6.

5. Lewthwaite, "Violence, Law and Community," *Essays in the History of Canadian Law*, Volume V, Jim Phillips, Tina Loo, and Susan

Lewthwaite eds. (Toronto: University of Toronto Press, 1983), 370; Oliver, *Terror to Evil-Doers: Prisons and Punishments in Nineteenth-Century Ontario* (Toronto: University of Toronto Press, 1998), 21.

6. Lewthwaite, "Violence, Law and Community," 385.
7. *Ibid.*, 369.
8. *Ibid.*
9. *Ibid.*, citing John Beverley Robinson to Harrison, 23 July 1841, box 1, Pre-Confederation correspondence, Provincial Secretary Records, RG 8-23, Archives of Ontario.
10. Weaver, *Crimes, Constables and Courts*, 39; citing Donald R. Beer, *Sir Allan Napier MacNab* (Hamilton: Dictionary of Hamilton Biography, 1984), 22–25.
11. *The Gore Gazette*, 24 August 1827.
12. W. L. Smith, *The Pioneers of Old Ontario* (Toronto: George N. Morang 1923), 320–22.

Chapter Six

1. Murray, *Colonial Justice: Justice, Morality, and Crime in the Niagara District, 1791–1849 (Toronto: University of Toronto Press, 2002)*, 23; Paul Romney, *Mr. Attorney: The Attorney General for Ontario in Court, Cabinet, and Legislature 1791–1899* (Toronto: University of Toronto Press, 1986).
2. This changed in 1857, when county prosecutors took over this role.
3. Talbot, *Justice in Early Ontario*, 26.
4. *Ibid.*
5. Romney, *Mr. Attorney: The Attorney General for Ontario in Court, Cabinet, and Legislature 1791–1899* (Toronto: University of Toronto Press, 1986), 37–53.
6. Talbot, *Justice in Early Ontario*, 27.
7. *Ibid.*
8. *Ibid.*, xiii–xvii; John Lownsbrough, "D'Arcy Boulton," *Dictionary of Canadian Biography*.
9. Pronounced "puny."
10. Romney, *Mr. Attorney: The Attorney General for Ontario in Court, Cabinet, and Legislature 1791–1899*, 11.
11. Talbot, *Justice in Early Ontario*, 24.
12. *Ibid.*

13. *Ibid.*, 23.
14. *Ibid.*, 25.
15. *Ibid.*; S. R. Mealing, "William Dummer Powell," *Dictionary of Canadian Biography*.
16. Romney, *The Administration of Justice in Ontario 1784–1900* (Winnipeg: University of Manitoba, Faculty of Law, Canadian Legal History Project, 1991), 1.
17. Murray, *Colonial Justice: Justice, Morality, and Crime in the Niagara District, 1791–1849 (Toronto: University of Toronto Press, 2002)*, 27–28.
18. *Ibid.*, 38–39.
19. Weaver, *Crimes, Constables and Courts*, 38.
20. Murray, *Colonial Justice: Justice, Morality, and Crime in the Niagara District, 1791–1849*, 24.
21. Romney, *The Administration of Justice in Ontario 1784–1900*, 13.
22. Murray, *Colonial Justice: Justice, Morality, and Crime in the Niagara District, 1791–1849*, 29–30, 37.
23. *Ibid.*, 26.
24. Talbot, *Justice in Early Ontario*, 28.
25. Keele, *A Brief View of the Township Laws Up To the Present Time: With a Treatise on the Law and Office of Constable, the Law Relative to Landlord and Tenant, Distress for Rent, Innkeepers, etc.* (Toronto?: 1835, 1884) (Toronto: W. J. Coates CIHM 10787), 147–48; *An Act to Declare What Fees Shall Be Received by Justices of the Peace for the Duties Therein Mentioned*, Statutes of Upper Canada, 4 William IV (1834) c.17.
26. John Clarke, "Mahlon Burwell," *Dictionary of Canadian Biography*.
27. This changed in 1857, when Clerks of the Peace were required to be Barristers at Law with at least three years at the bar of Upper Canada. Archives of Ontario, Archives Descriptive Database.
28. Talbot, *Justice in Early Ontario*, 39.
29. Josephine Phelan, "The Tar and Feather Case, Gore Assizes, August 1827," *Ontario History*, 68 No. 1 (1976), 17–23; William Canniff, *The Medical Profession in Upper Canada, 1783–1850 : An Historical Narrative with Original Documents Relating to the Profession, Including some Brief Biographies* (Toronto: W. Briggs, 1894) 588–590; T. Roy Woodhouse, *The History of the Town of Dundas*, Part One (Dundas, ON: Dundas Historical Society, 1965), 25.

30. Murray *Colonial Justice: Justice, Morality, and Crime in the Niagara District, 1791–1849*, 42–43.

31. Talbot, *Justice in Early Ontario*, 34.

32. *Ibid.*, 145–49; Beattie, *Attitudes Toward Crime and Punishment in Upper Canada 1830–1850: A Documentary Study* (Toronto: Working Paper of the Centre of Criminology, University of Toronto, 1977), 34; Murray, *Colonial Justice: Justice, Morality, and Crime in the Niagara District, 1791–1849*, 43.

33. Murray, *Colonial Justice: Justice, Morality, and Crime in the Niagara District, 1791–1849*, 43, 49–50; Archives Descriptive Database, Archives of Ontario; Romney, *The Administration of Justice in Ontario 1784–1900*, 6.

34. Murray, *Colonial Justice: Justice, Morality, and Crime in the Niagara District, 1791–1849*, 44, citing E. A. Cruikshank, "The Government of Upper Canada and Robert Gourlay," *Ontario History*, 23 (1926), 65–179.

35. Murray, *Colonial Justice: Justice, Morality, and Crime in the Niagara District, 1791–1849*, 48–51.

36. Murray, *Colonial Justice: Justice, Morality, and Crime in the Niagara District, 1791–1849*, 46, citing James Kerby to Major Hillier, 25 April 1827, Correspondence of the Civil Secretary (Upper Canada Sundries), RG5 A1, Volume 83, Pages 45455–58, Library and Archives Canada.

37. Resignation of Sheriff Joseph Ryerson, 30 October 1805, Charlotteville, correspondence of the Civil Secretary (Upper Canada Sundries) RG5 A1, Volume 1, Page 1478, Library and Archives Canada, film C-4503.

38. Talbot, *Justice in Early Ontario*, 34.

39. *The Macmillan Dictionary of Canadian Biography*, 4th ed. (Toronto: Macmillan of Canada, 1978); *The Canadian Biographical Dictionary and Portrait Gallery of Eminent and Self-Made Men, Ontario*, Volume One (Toronto: American Biographical Publishing Company, 1880), "Henry Ruttan" *www.cobourghistory.ca/ruttan.htm* (accessed 22 May 2010).

40. William Canniff, *History of the Province of Ontario (Upper Canada)* (Toronto : A.H. Hovey, 1872), 120–21.

41. Jones, *Pioneer crimes and punishments*, 87–98.

42. *Ibid.*, 87–98.

43. Oliver, *Terror to Evil-Doers*, 51.

44. *Ibid.*, 119–20.

45. *Ibid.*, 122.

46. *Ibid.*, 123.

47. Murray, *Colonial Justice: Justice, Morality, and Crime in the Niagara District, 1791–1849*, 64–65; Keele, *A Brief View of the Township Laws Up To the Present Time: With a Treatise on the Law and Office of Constable, the Law Relative to Landlord and Tenant, Distress for Rent, Innkeepers, etc.*, 15–16; Weaver, *Crimes, Constables and Courts*, 28.

48. Weaver, *Crimes, Constables and Courts*, 28; Murray, *Colonial Justice: Justice, Morality, and Crime in the Niagara District, 1791–1849*, 65.

49. Keele, *A Brief View of the Township Laws Up To the Present Time: With a Treatise on the Law and Office of Constable, the Law Relative to Landlord and Tenant, Distress for Rent, Innkeepers, etc.*, 15–16; Murray, *Colonial Justice: Justice, Morality, and Crime in the Niagara District, 1791–1849*, 65.

50. Weaver, *Crimes, Constables and Courts*, 28.

51. Murray, *Colonial Justice: Justice, Morality, and Crime in the Niagara District, 1791–1849*, 64–66.

52. *Ibid.*, 70.

53. *Ibid.*, 64; Keele, *A Brief View of the Township Laws Up To the Present Time: With a Treatise on the Law and Office of Constable, the Law Relative to Landlord and Tenant, Distress for Rent, Innkeepers, etc.*, 16–18.

54. Keele, *A Brief View of the Township Laws Up To the Present Time: With a Treatise on the Law and Office of Constable, the Law Relative to Landlord and Tenant, Distress for Rent, Innkeepers, etc.*, 18.

55. *Ibid.*, 17–18.

56. *Ibid.*, 19.

57. Murray, *Colonial Justice: Justice, Morality, and Crime in the Niagara District, 1791–1849*, 64.

58. Keele, *A Brief View of the Township Laws Up To the Present Time: With a Treatise on the Law and Office of Constable, the Law Relative to Landlord and Tenant, Distress for Rent, Innkeepers, etc.*, 127.

59. Murray, *Colonial Justice: Justice, Morality, and Crime in the Niagara District, 1791–1849*, 66.

60. Lewthwaite, "Violence, Law and Community," *Essays in the His-*

tory of Canadian Law, Volume V, Jim Phillips, Tina Loo, and Susan Lewthwaite eds. (Toronto: University of Toronto Press, 1983), citing Minute books, Newcastle District (Cobourg) Court of General Quarter Sessions of the Peace, and index to bylaws of Northumberland and Durham.

61. Murray, *Colonial Justice: Justice, Morality, and Crime in the Niagara District, 1791–1849*, 71, citing Account of Donald McDonald, 10 October 1836, Lincoln County Court of General Quarter Sessions of the Peace Records, RG 22 Series 372, Box 25, File 1, Archives of Ontario.

62. Murray, *Colonial Justice: Justice, Morality, and Crime in the Niagara District, 1791–1849*, 71–72.

63. Murray, *Colonial Justice: Justice, Morality, and Crime in the Niagara District, 1791–1849*, 71, citing Frances Ann Thompson, "Local Authority and District Autonomy: The Niagara Magistracy and Constabulary," PhD Thesis, (University of Ottawa, 1996), 197.

64. Marion MacRae and Anthony Adamson, *Cornerstones of Order: Courthouses And Town Halls Of Ontario, 1784–1914* (Toronto: The Osgoode Society, Clarke, Irwin, 1983), 67–68. The terms "high constable" and "high bailiff" were often used interchangeably as their duties were joined in one office.

65. Jones, *Pioneer Crimes and Punishments*, 152.

66. *Ibid.*, 169.

67. Peter Vronsky, "History of the Toronto Police," *www.russianbooks.org/crime/cp0.htm* (accessed 2 March 2009), part one; Romney, *The Administration of Justice in Ontario 1784–1900*, 21.

68. Romney, *The Administration of Justice in Ontario 1784–1900*, 21–22.

69. *Ibid.*, 21.

70. Vronsky, "History of the Toronto Police," citing Minutes, Toronto City Council, 12 November 1834, and 20 February 1837.

71. Romney, "A Struggle for Authority: Toronto Society and Politics in 1834," *Forging a Consensus: Historical Essays on Toronto*, Victor Loring Russell ed. (Toronto: University of Toronto Press, 1984), 19.

72. Paul Romney, "The Ordeal of William Higgins," *Ontario History*, 67 No. 2 (1975), 69–89; *Brown's Toronto General Directory*, 1856 (Toronto: W.R. Brown, 1856), 222, 369.

73. In 1850 jury panels stopped being selected by the sheriff and came

under the control of a committee of elected municipal officials. *An Act for the Consolidation and Amendment of the Laws Relative to Jurors, Juries and Inquests in That Part of This Province Called Upper Canada,* Statutes of Canada 13 & 14 Victoria c. 55 s. 11.

74. *An Act for the Relief of Menonists and Tunkers in Certain Cases,* Statutes of Upper Canada, 49 George III (1809), c. 6.

75. Murray, *Colonial Justice: Justice, Morality, and Crime in the Niagara District, 1791–1849,* 52–53.

76. Murray, *Colonial Justice: Justice, Morality, and Crime in the Niagara District, 1791–1849,* 54–55.

77. AO Archives Descriptive Database; Murray, *Colonial Justice: Justice, Morality, and Crime in the Niagara District, 1791–1849,* 62–63.

78. Murray, *Colonial Justice: Justice, Morality, and Crime in the Niagara District, 1791–1849,* 63, citing grand jury presentment, 16 March 1839, Lincoln County Court of General Quarter Sessions of the Peace Records, RG 22 Series 372, Box 34, File 6, Archives of Ontario; Oliver, *Terror to Evil-Doers,* 63.

79. Murray, *Colonial Justice: Justice, Morality, and Crime in the Niagara District, 1791–1849,* 62, citing grand jury presentment, 18 July 1828, Lincoln County Court of General Quarter Sessions of the Peace Records, RG 22 Series 372, Box 4, File 6, Archives of Ontario.

80. *An Act Establishing Trial by Jury in Upper Canada,* Statutes of Upper Canada, 32 George III (1792), c. 2 s. 1.

81. Murray, *Colonial Justice: Justice, Morality, and Crime in the Niagara District, 1791–1849,* 54–55.

82. Lewthwaite, "Violence, Law and Community," citing a newspaper report of the trial in the *Colonial Advocate,* 4 November 1824.

83. Archives Descriptive Database, Archives of Ontario.

84. Archives Descriptive Database, Archives of Ontario.

85. "Petition of Sundry Inhabitants Living in the Townships of Crowland, Wainfleet, Pelham and Thorold..." 18 March 1834, Lincoln County Court of General Quarter Sessions of the Peace Records, RG 22-372, Box 16, Folder 43, Archives of Ontario.

86. Murray, *Colonial Justice: Justice, Morality, and Crime in the Niagara District, 1791–1849,* 60–62.

87. Christopher Moore, *The Law Society of Upper Canada and Ontario's Lawyers, 1797–1997* (Toronto: University of Toronto Press, 1997), 37.

88. *Ibid.*, 58, 107; Wright, "Sedition in Upper Canada: Contested Legality," *Labour/Le Travail* 29 (Spring 1992), 52.

89. Wright, "Sedition in Upper Canada: Contested Legality," 52.

90. Moore, *The Law Society*, 39.

91. *Ibid.*, 46.

92. *Ibid.*, 86–87.

93. *Ibid.*, 48–50.

94. *Ibid.*, 25; Talbot, *Justice in Early Ontario*, 31–32 — There were sixteen licences issued before 1797 (David W. Smith, Richard Baines Tickell, Angus McDonell, James Clark, Allan McLean, Timothy Thompson, Robert I.D. Gray, Jacob Farrand, Nicholas Hagerman, William D. Powell, Alexander Stewart, Davenport Phelps, Charles J. Peters, W. Birdseye Peters, Samuel Sherwood, and probably Bartholomew C. Beardsley).

95. Moore, *The Law Society*, 13.

96. *An Act for Better Regulating the Practice of the Law*, Statutes of Upper Canada, 37 George III (1797), c. 8.

97. Riddell, "The Courts of Ontario," 22–23; *An Act for Better Regulating the Practice of the Law* Statutes of Upper Canada 37 George III (1797), c. 8.

98. G. Blaine Baker, "Legal Education in Upper Canada 1785–1889: The Law Society as Educator," *Essays in the History of Canadian Law*, Volume II, edited by David H. Flaherty (Toronto: University of Toronto Press, 1983), 80; Moore, *The Law Society,* 47.

99. Moore, *The Law Society*, 55.

100. Baker, "Legal Education," 81.

101. Moore, *The Law Society*, 89–90.

102. *Ibid.*, 90; Baker, "Legal Education," 70.

103. Baker, "Legal Education," 70.

104. Moore, *The Law Society*, 89.

105. Romney, *The Administration of Justice in Ontario 1784–1900*, 10.

106. *Ibid.*, 10.

107. Moore, *The Law Society*, 89–90.

108. Baker, "Legal Education," 113.

109. *Ibid.*, 114

110. Baker, "Legal Education," 114.

111. *Ibid.*, 85.

112. *Ibid.*, 51.

113. Orlo Miller, "For Honour's Sake," *Twenty Mortal Murders: Bizarre Murder Cases from Canada's Past* (Toronto: Macmillan of Canada, 1978), 54–62; *History of the County of Middlesex* (Toronto and London: W.A. and C.L. Godspeed, 1889; Reprint Belleville, ON: Mika Studio, 1972), 133–36.

114. Moore, *The Law Society*, 69.

Chapter Seven

1. Jones, *Pioneer Crimes and Punishments*, 7.

2. Talbot, *Justice in Early Ontario*, 167.

3. Romney, *The Administration of Justice in Ontario 1784–1900* (Winnipeg : University of Manitoba, Faculty of Law, Canadian Legal History Project, 1991), 21.

4. Niagara Regional Police Service, "A Brief History of the Service," *www.nrps.com/nrp/history.asp* (accessed 28 February 2010).

5. Vronsky, "History of the Toronto Police," Part Two.

6. "Ontario Provincial Police," *Wikipedia*, *en.wikipedia.org/wiki/ Ontario_Provincial_Police* (accessed 2 March 2010), citing Michael Barnes, *Policing Ontario: The OPP Today* (Erin, ON: Boston Mills Press, 1991).

7. Romney, *The Administration of Justice in Ontario 1784–1900*, 14.

8. Archives of Ontario, "A History of Ontario's Court System."

9. Romney, *The Administration of Justice in Ontario 1784–1900*, 13.

10. McKenna, "Women's Agency in Upper Canada," 351–54; MacRae and Adamson, *Cornerstones of Order*, 136.

11. Romney, *The Administration of Justice in Ontario 1784–1900*, 14.

12. Archives of Ontario, "A History of Ontario's Court System."

13. Archives of Ontario, "Draft Guide to the Criminal Justice Records at the Archives of Ontario," version 6.0 (April 2008), 23.

14. Archives of Ontario, "Draft Guide," 23–24.

15. Archives of Ontario, "A History of Ontario's Court System."

16. Oliver, *Terror to Evil-Doers*, 24–25.

17. Jones, *Pioneer Crimes and Punishments*, 7.

18. Romney, *The Administration of Justice in Ontario 1784–1900*, 20.

19. Talbot, *Justice in Early Ontario*, 167.

20. Romney, *The Administration of Justice in Ontario 1784–1900*, 20.

21. *Ibid.*
22. *Ibid.*
23. *Ibid.*, 13.
24. *An Act for the Consolidation and Amendment of the Laws Relative to Jurors, Juries and Inquests in That Part of This Province Called Upper Canada*, Statutes of Canada 13 & 14 Victoria c. 55 s. 11.
25. Murray, *Colonial Justice: Justice, Morality, and Crime in the Niagara District, 1791–1849 (Toronto: University of Toronto Press, 2002)*, 90–97, 103.

Chapter Eight

1. R. vs. Daniel Sullivan (*et al*), 21–23 November 1833, 19 February 1834, 6 July 1837, 3 January 1849, Minutes of the York County (Toronto) Court of General Quarter Sessions of the Peace, Archives of Ontario RG 22- 94.
2. Proceedings of the Mayor's Court, 2 June 1834 to 4 Sept 1838, RG7 E Box 1, pages 13, 23, 25–26, 33, 36, 64, 69–70, 75, 133–34, Toronto City Archives.
3. R vs. Daniel Sullivan, Minutes of the Home District Assize, 16 October 1837, Archives of Ontario, RG 22-134.
4. Kingston Penitentiary Punishment Book, 1835–1853 and Work Book, August 1837 to March 1840, Library and Archives Canada, RG73 C6 (R942-28-X-E).
5. Romney, "A Struggle for Authority: Toronto Society and Politics in 1834," *Forging a Consensus: Historical Essays on Toronto*, Victor Loring Russell ed. (Toronto: University of Toronto Press, 1984), 29, citing *Toronto Recorder* 15, 18 July 1835.

INDEX

grand jury, 54–55, 57, 150,
152–53
grand larceny, 65
Greneau, Mary, 53

H
Hagerman, Christopher, 130,
132
Halfpenny, Ellen, 27
Hamilton, 52
Hands, William, 141
Hathaway Farensworth,
Samuel, 23–25
Hesse District, 132
Higgins, Julia, 90
high constables, 148–49
High Court Judges records,
164–65
High Court of Justice of
the Supreme Court of
Ontario, 178
high treason, 96
Home District, 149–50
Home (Nassau) District
records, 191–92
Howard, Stephen, 137
Huron District records, 192

I
immigration, 15
imprisonment, 87, 97–109
purpose of, 107

indictable offences, 16–17
industrial school for girls (*see*
Ontario Industrial Refuge
for Girls)
industrial training school for
boys, 179
innkeepers, 17
intoxicated people, 100
investigation, 32–39
investigations, 45–47
trials, 84–86
investigative records, 39–47
Ireland, G. T. F., 137
Irish population, 18, 149
Irish women, 18

J
Jackson, William, 59
jail (*see* gaol)
jailer (*see* gaoler)
Johnstown District records,
192–93
Jones, Eleas, 137
Jones, John, 63–64
judges, 129
Chief Justice, 131
Puisne Justices, 131
juries, 150–58
grand , 54–55, 57, 150,
152–53
petty (petit) juries, 150,
153–55

OTHER GENEALOGIST'S
REFERENCE SHELF TITLES

Genealogical Standards of Evidence
A Guide for Family Historians
Brenda Dougall Merriman
978-1-55488-451-3

Genealogy and family history revolve around issues of identification. Genealogical evidence is the information — analyzed and evaluated — that allows us to identify an individual, and event in his or her life, or the relationship between individuals. This book will tell you about how the genealogical community developed standards of evidence and documentation, what those standards are, and how you can apply them to your own work.

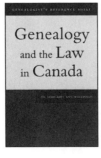

Genealogy and the Law in Canada
Dr. Margaret Ann Wilkinson
978-1-55488-452-0

The development of digital records and broad access to the web has revolutionized the ways in which genealogists approach their investigations — and has made it much easier to locate relevant information. The law, on the other hand, remains very connected to particular geographic locations. This book discusses the relevant laws — access to information, protection of personal data, and copyright — applicable to those working within Canada with materials that are located in Canada.